Modern Holiday

Deck the Halls with 18 Sewing Projects
Quilts, Stockings, Decorations & More

AMANDA  MURPHY

stashBOOKS®

an imprint of C&T Publishing

Text copyright © 2013 by Amanda Murphy

Photography and Artwork copyright © 2013 by C&T Publishing, Inc.

Publisher: Amy Marson

Creative Director: Gailen Runge

Art Director: Kristy Zacharias

Editor: Deb Rowden

Technical Editors: Priscilla Read and Gailen Runge

Cover/Book Designer: April Mostek

Production Coordinator: Jenny Davis

Production Editor: Joanna Burgarino

Illustrator: Amanda Murphy

Photo Assistant: Mary Peyton Peppo

Photography by Christina Carty-Francis and Diane Pedersen of C&T Publishing, Inc., unless otherwise noted

Published by Stash Books, an imprint of C&T Publishing, Inc., P.O. Box 1456, Lafayette, CA 94549

Library of Congress Cataloging-in-Publication Data

Murphy, Amanda, 1971-

 Modern holiday : deck the halls with 18 sewing projects - quilts, stockings, decorations & more / Amanda
Murphy.

    pages cm

 ISBN 978-1-60705-678-2 (soft cover)

1. Patchwork--Patterns. 2. Appliqué--Patterns. 3. Quilting--Patterns. 4. Christmas decorations. I. Title.

TT835.M846 2013

746.46--dc23

                           2012038745

Printed in China

10 9 8 7 6 5 4 3 2 1

Contents

I would like to thank...

My family: my husband, whose support has enabled me to pursue my creative endeavors; our daughter and son, who have helped with many of these projects; and my parents, who have always been my biggest and most enthusiastic supporters.

Acknowledgments

Grateful thanks go to Amy Marson, my editor Deb Rowden, and the staff at C&T Publishing, who believed in my vision of a modern Christmas quilting book and helped bring it to life.

Many companies in the quilting industry manufacture great products integral to making the projects in *Modern Holiday*. I was fortunate to sew with beautiful fabrics from Robert Kaufman Fabrics, Riley Blake Designs, Michael Miller Fabrics, and Moda Fabrics. (Specific designer information is listed under the main picture for each quilt, and I've included a Fabric Designer Blog Roll, page 141. Even if the fabric line pictured is no longer available, it is likely that these designers will have new, equally exciting fabric lines available.)

All projects were sewn on a Bernina 580e, a wonderful sewing and embroidery machine with unsurpassed stitch quality and with capabilities I am still discovering daily! Special thanks to Bernina of America and to Drusilla Munnell and the staff of Sew Much Fun, my local Bernina dealer and quilt shop in Gastonia, North Carolina, who have provided enthusiastic support in all my creative endeavors in this industry.

Aurifil, Sulky, the Warm Company, and Clover Needlecraft all provided their great products for these projects. You can find specifics about what I used in the instructions and reference company information in the Supplies and Sources section (page 142).

Last, I'd like to thank Deborah Norris of Deborah's Quilting in Gastonia, who quilted all the large projects in *Modern Holiday*. She has a wonderful ability to capture the style of a quilt design and translate that into playful, free-form quilting. Deborah's work elevates a project to an entirely new level of design. I am always so excited to drive up to her studio and see my newly quilted projects for the first time!

Joy

The holidays are a time to create special memories for the people you love. Spread that joy throughout the year with a wide variety of fun and whimsical projects!

Introduction . . . .

What sights, smells, sounds, and tastes evoke the Christmas holidays for you? The first thing that comes to my mind is color— lots of it! The projects here are inspired by twinkling lights, candles, colorful ornaments, and playful wrapping paper. Of course, homemade sugar cookies served with a little hot chocolate with whipped cream never fail to get those creative juices flowing. So turn on that holiday music and start sewing!

It is said that the pleasure of presents is really in the giving. This is particularly true with handmade items. Making gifts for others with thread and needle gives us time to reflect—to stop and enjoy our lives and the people in them.

In *Modern Holiday* you will find some projects that are specific to Christmas, like the playful stockings (page 103) and the Advent calendar (page 95). You'll also find some more general projects that capture the exuberance of the season but can be sewn in a wide variety of prints and displayed throughout the year. *Modern Madness*

(page 49) and *Crossroads* (page 25) are two such versatile patterns.

While this book is intended for intermediate sewists, none of the techniques are difficult. Basic blocks, such as half-square triangles and Flying Geese, are the foundations for the projects in this book. Applying these techniques in a variety of ways yields dramatically different results. For *Trimming the Tree* (page 73), I made simple large quilt blocks, and then assembled and appliquéd them onto a patterned background.

Don't be afraid to use my designs as a jumping-off point. What about sewing *Trimming the Tree* in patterned prints on a solid background, or whipping up *Bloom* (page 63) in your favorite spring collection? Unleash your own creativity, and let your own personal style take these projects to an entirely new level. So are you ready? Pull out your most colorful prints and start assembling your own *Modern Holiday*!

Happy sewing!

Amanda

QUILT FOR THE

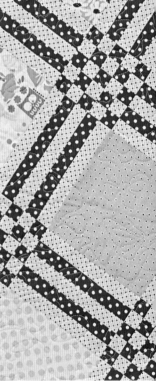

Holidays

Holiday Squares

Finished Blocks:
12″ × 12″

Finished Quilt:
58″ × 72″

Fabrics shown are from Funky Christmas and other holiday collections by Michael Miller Fabrics.

Pieced by
Amanda Murphy

Quilted by
Deborah Norris

Whip up this fun project in your most vibrant collection of Christmas fabrics! Try throwing some coordinating solids into the mix to make the feature prints stand out. It is interesting to see how different the blocks look depending on fabric placement. Don't try to plan too much— the surprises make this quilt fun!

MATERIALS

Block fabrics: 12 fat quarters

Accent squares fabric: ¼ yard

Sashing fabric: ¾ yard

Inner border fabric: 1¾ yards (*A little of this fabric is in each of the blocks also; a white or light fabric that reads as a solid is a good choice.*)

Middle border fabric: ½ yard

Outer border fabric: 1¼ yards

Binding fabric: ⅝ yard

Backing fabric: 5 yards

Batting: 66″ × 80″ (Warm & Natural batting by the Warm Company)

CUTTING INSTRUCTIONS

WOF = width of fabric

From each fat quarter fabric:
Turn *lengthwise*, as shown in the cutting diagram, and cut 2 strips 2½″. Set aside.

Turn fabric *widthwise* and cut 1 strip 5¼″ wide, 1 strip 4½″ wide, and 2 strips 2⅞″ wide. Subcut into 2 squares 5¼″ × 5¼″, 1 square 4½″ × 4½″, and 8 squares 2⅞″ × 2⅞″.

From accent squares fabric:
Cut 2 strips 2½″ × WOF. Subcut into 20 squares 2½″ × 2½″.

From sashing fabric:
Cut 2 strips 12½″ × WOF. Subcut into 31 strips 2½″ × 12½″.

From inner border fabric:
Cut 20 strips 2½″ × WOF. Cut 12 of these strips in half to use for the blocks.

From middle border fabric:
Cut 7 strips 1½″ × WOF.

From outer border fabric:
Cut 8 strips 4¼″ × WOF.

From binding fabric:
Cut 7 strips 2¼″ × WOF.

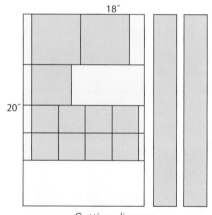

Cutting diagram

Block Assembly

1. Separate all the 5¼″ × 5¼″ and 2⅞″ × 2⅞″ squares into 2 piles, with 1 large square and 4 small squares of each print in each pile.

2. Starting with the first pile, use 1 square 5¼″ × 5¼″ and 4 contrasting identical squares 2⅞″ × 2⅞″ to make 4 Flying Geese units. Follow the instructions in the Easy Flying Geese sidebar (page 15) and press seams open. Repeat with all remaining squares 5¼″ × 5¼″ and 2⅞″ × 2⅞″ in the first pile to complete Flying Geese. Set the pile aside.

3. Repeat with the second pile of 5¼″ × 5¼″ and 2⅞″ × 2⅞″ squares, making sure to pair the prints differently from those in Step 2.

4. Join 2 Flying Geese together, 1 from each pile, making sure to choose a unit with a "goose" that is cut from the same fabric as the other unit's "sky," as shown. Press toward the fat quarter "goose." Repeat to complete 4 identical Flying Geese units. **FIGURE ❶**

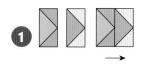

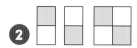

5. Repeat Step 4 with remaining Flying Geese.

6. Join a 2½″ × WOF strip from the fat quarters to a 2½″ × WOF inner border strip that has been cut in half. Press seams toward the fat quarter fabric. Repeat to make an identical strip set. Subcut these sets to make 8 units 2½″ wide. Join these units together in pairs to make 4 four-square units, as shown. **FIGURE ❷**

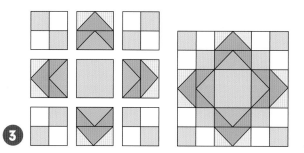

7. Repeat Step 6 with remaining fat quarter strips 2½″ × WOF to make 4 four-square units in each print.

8. Join 4 Flying Geese units with 4 four-square units and 1 square 4¼″ × 4¼″ to make 1 quilt block. Match the 4¼″ × 4¼″ square with the fat quarter fabric in the four-square units, placing the four-square units as oriented in the illustration. When joining rows, press seams toward the Flying Geese blocks. **FIGURE ❸**

9. Repeat Step 8 to make 12 quilt blocks.

Quilt Assembly

1. Following the assembly diagram, lay out the blocks, sashing, and accent squares to form the center of the quilt top.

2. Join 4 accent squares with 3 sashing rectangles to form sashing rows, pressing seams toward the sashing. Make 5 sashing rows.

3. Join 4 sashing rectangles with 3 blocks to form block rows, pressing seams toward the sashing. Make 4 block rows.

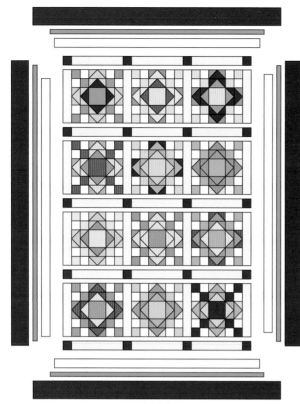

Assembly diagram

4. Join rows.

5. My quilt top at this point was 44½″ × 58½″. Measure your quilt and adjust border measurements accordingly.

6. Piece 2 inner border strips 2½″ × 58½″ and sew onto each side of the quilt top. Piece 2 inner border strips 2½″ × 48½″ and sew onto the top and bottom of the quilt top.

7. Piece 2 middle border strips 1½″ × 62½″ and sew onto each side of the quilt top. Piece 2 middle border strips 1½″ × 50½″ and sew onto the top and bottom of the quilt top.

8. Piece 2 outer border strips 4¼″ × 64½″ and sew onto each side of the quilt top. Piece 2 outer border strips 4¼″ × 58″ and sew onto the top and bottom of the quilt top.

Finishing

1. Divide backing fabric into 2 lengths. Cut 1 piece lengthwise to make 2 narrow panels. Join 1 narrow panel to each side of wide panel. Press seams open.

2. Layer backing, batting, and quilt top. Quilt as desired.

3. Join the binding strips 2¼″ × WOF into 1 continuous piece for binding. Press, folding in half lengthwise. Sew binding to quilt.

Easy Flying Geese

Many great templates are on the market today to make Flying Geese quickly and accurately. (If you are using a template, adjust the Cutting Instructions accordingly.) If you prefer not to use a template, here is a simple method to make 4 Flying Geese (2˝ × 4˝ finished, not including seam allowances).

1. Cut 1 square 5¼˝ × 5¼˝ for the geese and 4 matching squares 2⅞˝ × 2⅞˝ for the "sky." Draw a diagonal line on the wrong side of each sky fabric. Following the illustration, align 2 fabric squares 2⅞˝ × 2⅞˝ on the opposite corners of the background square 5¼˝ × 5¼˝, right sides together. Stitch a scant ¼˝ away from both sides of the drawn diagonal line.

2. Cut along drawn line. Open out the triangles. Press seams open or toward the sky fabric, as specified in the project's directions. Align another square 2⅞˝ × 2⅞˝ on the remaining unsewn corner of these units, right sides together. Sew a scant ¼˝ away from both sides of the drawn line. Cut along the drawn line. Open out the triangle and press. Trim unit to 2½˝ × 4½˝ if needed.

FIGURES ❶ – ❹

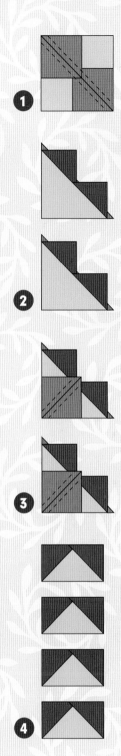

Christmas Gifts

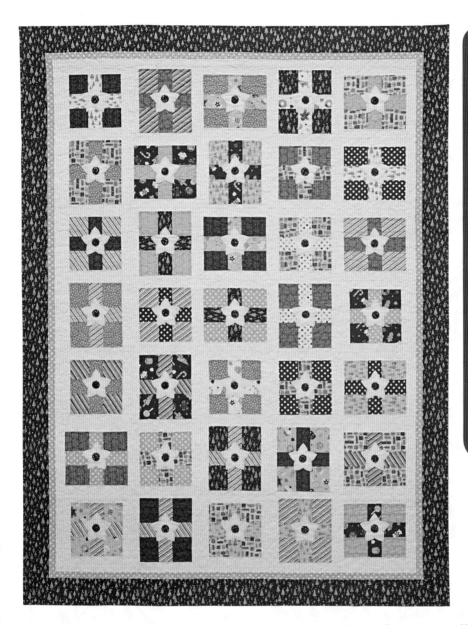

Finished Blocks:
10″ × 10″

Finished Quilt:
62″ × 82″

Fabrics shown are from the Christmas Candy Collection by Doodlebug Design for Riley Blake Designs, accented with polka dot prints by Darlene Zimmerman for Robert Kaufman Fabrics and by Deb Strain for Moda Fabrics.

Pieced by
Amanda Murphy

Quilted by
Deborah Norris

Start with 10″ squares and wrap up some holiday fun! Top off these colorful Christmas presents with a beautiful star flower bow. For a different look, you can use buttons instead of yo-yos. The appliqué bows used in *Holiday Wreaths* (page 33) or blossoms made from Clover's large Kanzashi Flower Makers are also fun options.

MATERIALS

Presents fabric: 53 squares 10″ × 10″

Flower bows fabric: 1 yard of 1 fabric for the star flowers and ½ yard of a contrasting print for the yo-yo flower centers

Background fabric: 3¼ yards

Inner border fabric: ½ yard

Outer border fabric: 1⅛ yards (2 yards for a directional print)

Binding fabric: ¾ yard

Backing fabric: 5 yards

Paper-backed fusible web: 2 yards

Tear-away stabilizer: 2 yards

Appliqué thread: 12-, 28-, or 30-weight cotton thread

Batting: 70″ × 90″ (Warm & White batting by the Warm Company)

Clover small green "Quick" Yo-Yo Maker #8700 (optional but highly recommended)

CUTTING INSTRUCTIONS
WOF = width of fabric

From block fabric:
Take 35 squares 10″ × 10″ of the presents fabric. Cut each into 2 rectangles 4¼″ × 10″. These will be the wrapping paper on your presents.

Subcut each of the remaining 18 squares 10″ × 10″ into 4 rectangles 2½″ × 10″. These will be the ribbons that wrap around the presents.

From background fabric:
Cut 4 strips 9½″ × WOF and 4 strips 11″ × WOF. Subcut into 70 rectangles 2″ × 9½″ and 70 rectangles 2″ × 11″.

Cut 8 strips 1½″ × WOF for the sashing.

From inner border fabric:
Cut 8 strips 1½″ × WOF.

From outer border fabric:
Cut 8 strips 4¼″ × WOF. *If you are using a directional print, cut 4 strips and then turn the fabric lengthwise to cut the remaining strips.*

From binding fabric:
Cut 8 strips 2¼″ × WOF.

Block Assembly

1. Insert a contrasting rectangle 2½″ × 10″ between 2 matching rectangles 4¼″ × 10″. Join pieces as shown, pressing seams toward center rectangle. **FIGURE ❶**

2. Turn block sideways and cut into 2 rectangles 5″ × 10″. Insert a rectangle 2½″ × 10″ that matches the "ribbon" that was inserted in Step 1 between the 2 units. Join pieces as shown, pressing seams toward center rectangle. **FIGURE ❷**

3. Repeat Steps 1 and 2 to form 35 presents. Trim some of these blocks down to rectangles 8″ × 9½″ and others down to squares 8″ × 8″, centering the "ribbon." (My quilt had 12 cut 8″ × 8″ and 23 cut 8″ × 9½″.)

4. Join a background rectangle 2″ × 9½″ onto the long sides of the rectangles as shown, pressing seams toward presents. Trim ends of these rectangles flush with block, if necessary. **FIGURE 3**

5. Join a background rectangle 2″ × 11″ onto the top and bottom of these units as shown, pressing seams toward presents. **FIGURE 4**

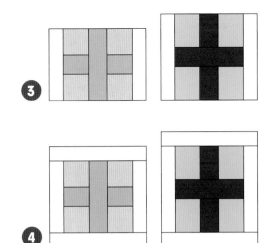

Bow Assembly

1. Trace the Star Flower Template onto the smooth side of the fusible web 35 times. Cut out the central portion of each star about ¼″ from its edge so that you will be left with only a little fusible web in your finished quilt.

2. Fuse to *wrong side* of the star flower fabric. Cut out star flowers.

3. Remove paper backing from flowers and fuse a flower onto each block, following the assembly diagram, at the intersection of the ribbons. (Note the different orientations of the block—the star flower is pointed up on each block.)

4. Back with tear-away stabilizer and machine appliqué each flower onto a block, using a buttonhole or zigzag stitch and following tips in the Fusible Appliqué sidebar (page 22).

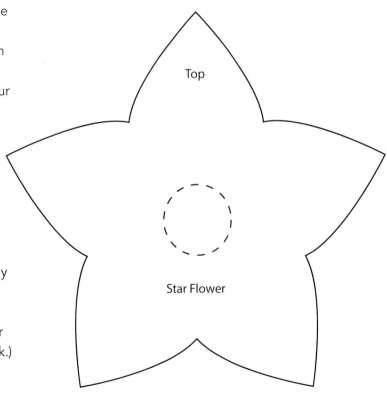

Top

Star Flower

5. Tear off stabilizer and cut excess fabric from behind each flower, being careful not to cut the flower itself.

6. Trim all blocks to squares 10½″ × 10½″.

7. Make 35 yo-yos using the Clover "Quick" Yo-Yo Maker and a strong thread, like buttonhole thread. (If you don't have a Clover "Quick" Yo-Yo Maker, cut out 35 circles 2¾″, take a large ¼″ running stitch around the edge, turning under the fabric ¼″ as you go. Pull tight, knot, and bury the threads.)

8. Refer to the photographs on the left and attach a yo-yo to the center of each star flower. Thread a needle with thread that matches the color of the yo-yo. Knot the end of the thread, leaving at least 3″ of thread beyond the knot. Come up through the *wrong side* of the block through the flower center. Come up through the center of the yo-yo and go back down through the center of both the yo-yo and the block. Make a knot with the tail end of your thread, but don't cut the thread. Travel between the layers to a point at the yo-yo's edge. Come up through the edge of the yo-yo. Make a tiny backstitch and go back down through all layers. Travel about ¼″ along the yo-yo's edge and come back up. Make a tiny backstitch. Proceed to sew all around the yo-yo, making tiny backstitches about ¼″ apart. When you arrive back at your starting place, travel back to the tail end of your thread through all fabric layers and make another knot. Trim threads to about ½″. Repeat to add a yo-yo to each block. *(You can also attach the yo-yos using tack stitches on your machine if you prefer.)*

Quilt Assembly

1. Following the assembly diagram lay out 7 rows of 5 blocks each to form the center of the quilt top, making sure the star flower bow is oriented correctly.

2. Join blocks into rows. Press seams so they alternate in each row.

3. Join rows.

4. My quilt top at this point was 50½″ × 70½″. Measure your quilt and adjust the following border measurements accordingly.

5. Piece 2 inner sashing strips 1½″ × 70½″ and sew onto each side of the quilt top. Piece 2 inner sashing strips 1½″ × 52½″ and sew onto the top and bottom of the quilt top.

6. Piece 2 inner border strips 1½″ × 72½″ and sew onto each side of the quilt top. Piece 2 inner border strips 1½″ × 54½″ and sew onto the top and bottom of the quilt top.

7. Piece 2 outer border strips 4¼″ × 74½″ and sew onto each side of the quilt top. Piece 2 outer border strips 4¼″ × 62″ and sew onto the top and bottom of the quilt top.

Assembly diagram

Finishing

1. Divide the backing fabric into 2 lengths. Cut 1 piece lengthwise to make 2 narrow panels. Join 1 narrow panel to each side of the wide panel. Press seams open.

2. Layer backing, batting, and quilt top. Quilt as desired.

3. If you are choosing to use flowers or three-dimensional bows, attach them by hand.

4. Join the 2¼˝-wide binding strips into 1 continuous piece for binding. Press, folding in half lengthwise. Sew binding to quilt.

Fusible Appliqué

1. Trace your shape onto the smooth side of the paper-backed fusible web.

2. Cut excess fusible from the inside shape. Fuse to the back of the appliqué fabric.

3. Cut out appliqué, remove paper, and fuse onto the block.

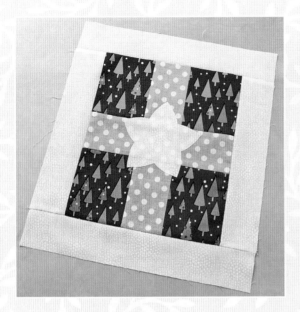

For a fun, professional-looking finish, use a heavyweight thread, like Aurifil's 12- or 30-weight or Sulky's 12- or 28-weight cottons with a large top-stitching needle (and a matching 50-weight cotton thread in the bobbin) when securing fusible appliqué shapes to your project.

After fusing the shapes in place, back the block with tear-away stabilizer. Choose a blanket-style stitch and loosen the thread tension so the bobbin thread does not pop to the top. On my Bernina 580e, I used the #1329 blanket stitch with the top tension lowered to 1.5. *Note: If your machine doesn't have a blanket-style stitch, you can use a narrow zigzag stitch with a lighter-weight thread.* Bring both threads to the top of the fabric. While holding them to the side, begin to sew around the shape.

After reaching the starting point, lift the presser foot and pull the piece out from the machine, clipping the threads so that the tails are about 4″ long.

Thread all the tails into a chenille needle with a large eye and bring them to the back of the block. Tie a knot close to the fabric. Rip off the stabilizer and trim the excess fabric from the back of the appliqué to get rid of bulk.

Crossroads

Finished Blocks:
8″ × 8″

Finished Quilt:
65″ × 90″

Fabrics shown are from the Blue and Aqua collection by Michael Miller Fabrics.

Pieced by
Amanda Murphy

Quilted by
Deborah Norris

Dynamic sashing strips and Checkerboard blocks enhance your favorite feature fabrics in this modern design. Choose sashing fabrics that read as solids to really make the blocks pop!

MATERIALS

Light sashing and checkerboard fabric:
2¾ yards

Dark sashing, checkerboard,
and inner border fabric: 2¼ yards

Feature fabrics: 31 squares 8½″ × 8½″

Inner border fabric: ½ yard

Outer border and binding fabric: 2 yards

Lightweight fusible interfacing: ¾ yard

Backing fabric: 5¾ yards

Batting: 73″ × 98″ (Warm & Natural
batting by the Warm Company)

CUTTING INSTRUCTIONS

WOF = width of fabric

From light sashing and checkerboard fabric:
Cut 56 strips 1½″ × WOF.

From dark sashing and checkerboard fabric:
Cut 52 strips 1½″ × WOF. Set 8 of these strips
aside for inner border.

From outer border and binding fabric:
Cut 9 strips 4¼″ × WOF for outer border.

Cut 9 strips 2¼″ × WOF for binding.*

From lightweight fusible interfacing:
Cut 14 strips 1½″ × WOF.

** If continuous bias binding is desired, please consult
my blog at amandamurphydesign.blogspot.com or go to
tinyurl.com/quiltmaking-basics and download the PDF
"How to Finish Your Quilt."*

Block Assembly

1. Join 3 light sashing strips to 2 dark sashing strips as shown, pressing seams toward the dark strips. Repeat to make 16 strip sets. Subcut strip sets into 60 units 8½″ wide and 64 units 1½″ wide. **FIGURE ❶**

2. Join 3 dark sashing strips 1½″ × WOF to 2 light sashing strips as shown, pressing seams toward the dark strips. Repeat to make 4 strip sets. Subcut strip sets into 96 units 1½″ wide. **FIGURE ❷**

3. Join 2 units 1½″ wide from Step 1 and 3 units 1½″ wide from Step 2 together to make a checkerboard square, as shown. Repeat to make 32 checkerboard blocks. Press seams toward rows 1, 3, and 5. **FIGURE ❸**

Quilt Assembly

1. Following assembly diagram 1, lay out the checkerboard, sashing, and feature fabric blocks to form the center of the quilt. **FIGURE ❹**

2. Join blocks into rows, pressing seams toward square units. Make sure that the raw edge of the short row extends ¼″ beyond the seam of the longer row. Press all seams toward square units.

3. Join rows.

4. Trim the quilt center down to size by cutting ¼″ out from the corner points of the blocks, as shown. The dotted line indicates the seamline—**not** the cutting line! Cut ¼″ out from dotted line. **FIGURE ❺**

5. Turn the quilt top over. Being careful not to stretch the edges of the quilt, apply interfacing along the perimeter, flush with the quilt top's edge. This will stabilize the bias edges that are exposed before adding borders.

6. The center of my quilt top after trimming was 55½″ × 80½″. Measure yours and adjust the following border measurements accordingly.

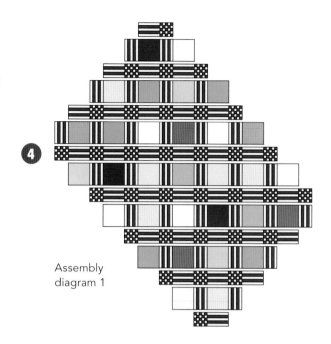

❹

Assembly diagram 1

❺

7. Piece 2 inner border strips 1½″ × 80½″ and sew onto each side of the quilt top. Piece 2 inner border strips 1½″ × 57½″ and sew onto the top and bottom of the quilt top.

8. Piece 2 outer border strips 4¼″ × 82½″ and sew onto each side of the quilt top. Piece 2 outer border strips 4¼″ × 65″ and sew onto the top and bottom of the quilt top. **FIGURES** **6**

6

Assembly diagram 2

Finishing

1. Divide backing fabric into 2 lengths. Cut 1 piece lengthwise to make 2 narrow panels. Join 1 narrow panel to each side of the wide panel. Press seams open.

2. Layer backing, batting, and quilt top. Quilt as desired.

3. Join the 2¼″-wide binding strips into 1 continuous piece for binding. Press, folding in half lengthwise. Sew binding to quilt. Enjoy!

Let the Quilt Design Inspire a Unique Backing!

Frequently, you will have leftover scraps from making the top of the quilt. Let those scraps, and the quilt design itself, inspire a fun backing for your piece. Lay out your materials on a design wall, cutting them into strips if necessary, to piece a backing that reflects the personality of the quilt top. This is the perfect time to add a label into the mix as well!

Holiday Wreaths

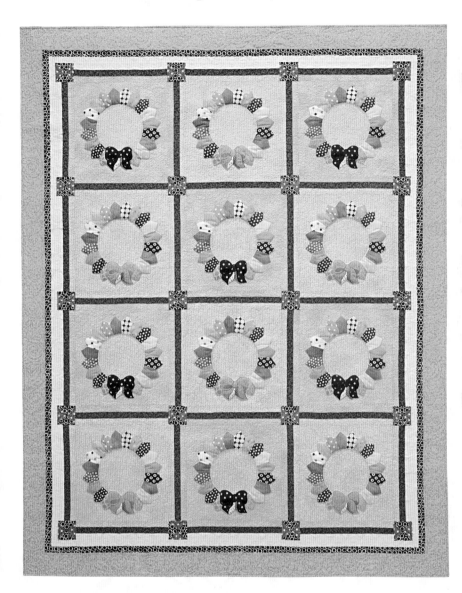

Finished Blocks:
15″ × 15″

Dresden Plates:
13½″

Finished Quilt:
69″ × 87″

Fabrics shown are from Patrick Lose, Monaluna, Piece O' Cake Designs, and other various neutral collections by Robert Kaufman Fabrics.

Pieced by
Amanda Murphy

Quilted by
Deborah Norris

Traditional Dresden blocks are turned into wreaths in this festive holiday quilt. Use an additional trapunto technique for added dimension and adorn each wreath with an appliqué bow. This is a great project to use the scraps in your collection!

MATERIALS

Very light background fabric: 2⅔ yards (choose a nondirectional print that reads as a solid)

Light background fabric: 2¼ yards (choose a nondirectional print that reads as a solid)

Accent squares fabric: ½ yard of 2 different prints

Sashing bars fabric: ⅞ yard

Dresden Plate fabrics: ¼ yard of 20 fabrics

Bow fabrics: ¼ yard each of a medium blue, dark blue, medium red, and dark red

Inner border fabric: ⅞ yard

Middle border fabric: ½ yard

Outer border and binding fabric: 1¾ yards

Appliqué thread: 12-, 28-, or 30-weight cotton thread (I used 28-weight Aurifil thread.)

Paper-backed fusible web: 3 yards

Tear-away stabilizer: 1 yard

Lite Steam-A-Seam 2 paper-backed ¼″ fusible tape: 1 roll

Backing fabric: 5⅓ yards

Batting: 77″ × 95″ (Warm & Natural batting by the Warm Company)

Dresden Plate ruler (*optional but highly recommended*): Easy Dresden by Darlene Zimmerman

Optional trapunto materials: High-loft batting (crib size)

YLI Wash-A-Way thread

CUTTING INSTRUCTIONS

WOF = width of fabric

From very light background fabric:
Cut 3 strips 16″ × WOF. Subcut into 6 squares 16″ × 16″.

Cut 13 strips 1½″ × WOF.

From light background fabric:
Cut 3 strips 16″ × WOF. Subcut into 6 squares 16″ × 16″.

Cut 16 strips 1½″ × WOF. Set remaining fabric aside.

From both accent squares fabrics:
Cut 2 strips 4¾″ × WOF. Subcut into 10 squares 4¾″ × 4¾″.

From sashing bars fabric:
Cut 17 strips 1½″ × WOF.

From Dresden Plate fabrics:
Cut into strips 5½″ × WOF. From strips, cut 240 wedges using your Dresden Plate ruler or the Dresden Plate Template.

From inner border fabric:
Cut 16 strips 1½″ × WOF.

From middle border fabric:
Cut 8 strips 1½″ × WOF.

From outer border and binding fabric:
Cut 8 strips 4¼″ × WOF for outer border.

Cut 9 strips 2¼″ × WOF for binding.*

* If continuous bias binding is desired, please consult my blog at amandamurphydesign.blogspot.com or go to tinyurl.com/quiltmaking-basics and download the PDF "How to Finish Your Quilt."

Block Assembly

1. Fold your Dresden Plate pieces in half *lengthwise, right sides together,* and sew across the wider end of the blade as shown, using a ¼″ seam allowance and backstitching on both ends of the seam. Clip the seam allowance of the folded corner to reduce bulk. Finger-press seam open and turn right side out. Press. Repeat to make 240 Dresden blades. **FIGURE ❶**

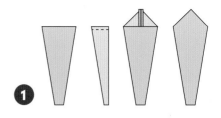

2. Sew the sides of 20 blades together to form a Dresden Plate. Fuse short pieces of fusible tape onto the outside edges of the wrong side of the plate. Remove tape and center the entire plate onto a very light 16″ × 16″ background square. Fuse. Attach using an invisible hem stitch or narrow appliqué stitch with matching thread. Repeat to make 6 very light blocks.

3. Repeat Step 2 to make 6 more Dresden Plates and appliqué them to the 6 light 16″ × 16″ background squares.

4. Draw 12 circles 7½″ onto the smooth side of the paper-backed fusible web. Cut out the central portion of each circle about ¼″ from its edge so that you will be left with only a little fusible in your finished quilt. Fuse each circle onto the wrong side of the remaining very light background fabric. Cut out circles. Remove paper and fuse each to the center of a Dresden Plate block. Machine appliqué each wreath center, using a blanket or zigzag stitch and following tips in the Fusible Appliqué sidebar (page 22). (Stabilizer is not needed because the Dresden Plates will provide stability.) Cut excess fabric from behind each wreath center, being careful to not cut the wreath center.

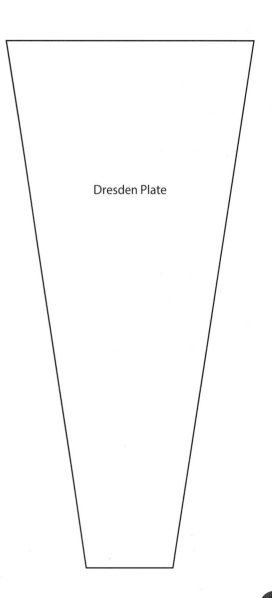

Dresden Plate

5. Using the same fusible appliqué technique, trace the outer black line of the Bow Template onto the smooth side of the paper-backed fusible web. Cut out the central portion of the fusible. Fuse the remaining portion to the wrong side of dark red bow fabric. Repeat with the inner red line shapes, fusing medium red fabrics. Remove paper from the medium red pieces and fuse to the dark red piece to form a bow. Repeat to make 6 red bows.

6. Repeat Step 5 with the medium and dark blue fabrics to make 6 blue bows.

7. Fuse all of one color of bow to the very light Dresden Plate blocks and all of the other color bow to the light Dresden Plate blocks, making sure that the bows come no closer than ½˝ to the edge of the blocks.

8. Following Fusible Appliqué directions (page 22), back the bow area with tear-away stabilizer and secure with a blanket stitch. Remove stabilizer.

9. Trim all blocks to 15½˝ × 15½˝.

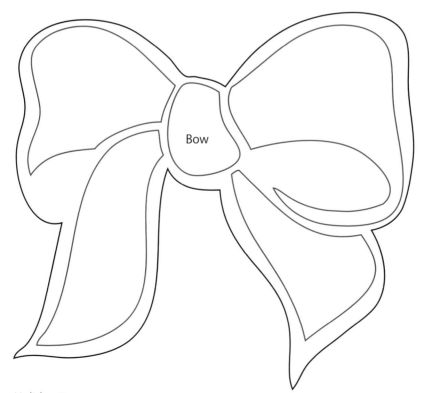

Bow

Optional Trapunto Technique

1. Thread your machine with YLI Wash-A-Way thread on the upper spool and neutral 50-weight cotton thread on the bobbin. Back each block with a square 15″ × 15″ of high-loft batting. Free-motion quilt around both the inner and outer wreath edge. Turn the block over and cut away excess batting. (Avoid ironing the trapunto area so as not to melt the batting.)

2. After the quilt is finished, wash your quilt or spray the water-soluble thread with water to dissolve.

Accent Square Assembly

1. Draw a diagonal line on the wrong side of just 1 color of the 4¾″ × 4¾″ accent squares. Place it right sides together with the contrasting color 4¾″ × 4¾″ accent square and sew ¼″ away from both sides of the drawn line. Cut apart on the original drawn line. Press seams toward darker fabric. Repeat with remaining accent squares. **FIGURE ➋**

2. Place 2 of these units right sides together, making sure that the seams lock and that contrasting fabrics are opposite each other. Draw a diagonal line on the wrong side of these units. Sew ¼″ away from both sides of the drawn line. Cut apart on the original drawn line and press seams open. Trim block to 3½″ × 3½″. Repeat to make 20 accent squares. **FIGURE ➌**

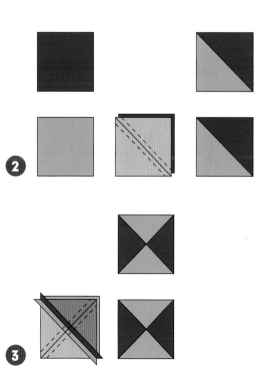

Sashing Assembly

1. Join 1 very light 1½˝ × WOF background strip to 1 sashing bar strip 1½˝ × WOF, pressing seams toward sashing bar. Join a light background strip to the other side of the sashing bar as shown, pressing seams toward sashing bar. Repeat to make 9 strip sets. Subcut strip sets into 17 units 15½˝ wide. **FIGURE ❹**

2. Join 1 very light 1½˝ × WOF background strip to 1 sashing bar strip 1½˝ × WOF, pressing seams toward the sashing bar. Join an inner border strip to the other side of the sashing bar as shown, pressing seams toward the sashing bar. Repeat to make 4 strip sets. Subcut strip sets into 7 units 15½˝ wide. **FIGURE ❺**

3. Join 1 light 1½˝ × WOF background strip to 1 sashing bar strip 1½˝ × WOF, pressing seams toward sashing bar. Join an inner border strip to the other side of the sashing bar as shown, pressing seams toward sashing bar. Repeat to make 4 strip sets. Subcut the strip sets into 7 units 15½˝ wide. **FIGURE ❻**

Quilt Assembly

1. Following the assembly diagram, lay out the Dresden Plate, accent square, and sashing blocks to form the center of the quilt.

2. Join blocks into rows, pressing all seams toward rectangular units.

3. Join rows.

4. The center of my quilt top was 57½˝ × 75½˝. Measure yours and adjust the following border measurements accordingly.

5. Piece 2 inner border strips 1½˝ × 75½˝ and sew onto each side of the quilt top. Piece 2 inner border strips 1½˝ × 59½˝ and sew onto the top and bottom of the quilt top.

6. Piece 2 middle border strips 1½˝ × 77½˝ and sew onto each side of the quilt top. Piece 2 middle border strips 1½˝ × 61½˝ and sew onto the top and bottom of the quilt top.

7. Piece 2 outer border strips 4¼˝ × 79½˝ and sew onto each side of the quilt top. Piece 2 outer border strips 4¼˝ × 69˝ and sew onto the top and bottom of the quilt top.

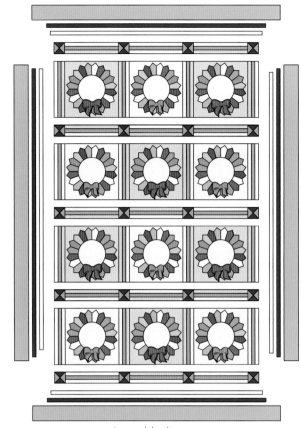

Assembly diagram

Finishing

1. Divide backing fabric into 2 lengths. Cut 1 piece lengthwise to make 2 narrow panels. Join 1 narrow panel to each side of the wide panel. Press seams open.

2. Layer backing, batting, and quilt top. Quilt as desired.

3. Join the binding strips 2¼˝ × WOF into 1 continuous piece for binding. Press, folding in half lengthwise. Sew binding to quilt.

For a fun label, sew up an extra wreath block for the back of the quilt!

Holiday Forest

Finished Quilt:
63˝ × 76˝

Fabrics shown are Ready Set Snow by Moda Fabrics and a wide range of neutrals by Robert Kaufman Fabrics, including those by Patrick Lose.

Pieced by
Amanda Murphy

Quilted by
Deborah Norris

Plant a holiday forest one tree at a time! Appliqué the snowflakes in pearly white metallic thread to really make your design sparkle.

MATERIALS

Trees: 3 yards total of assorted light green and aqua prints (*Make sure at least 4 pieces are at least 21½″ in length for the large trees.*)

Tree block background fabrics: 2⅓ yards green fabric

Tree trunks: ⅓ yard

Snowflakes: ½ yard white fabric

Snowflake background fabrics: ½ yard each of 2 fabrics

Sashing fabric: 1¾ yards

Top and bottom border fabric: ½ yard

Binding fabric: ¾ yard

Paper-backed fusible web: 1 yard

Stabilizer: 1 yard Sulky Tear-Easy

Template material: quilting plastic, hard board, or freezer paper

Backing fabric: 5 yards

Metallic appliqué thread for appliqué: Yenmet #110-AN1

Batting: 71″ × 84″ (Warm & White batting by the Warm Company)

CUTTING INSTRUCTIONS

WOF = width of fabric

Enlarge Tree and Tree Background Templates 250% and trace onto quilting plastic, hard board, or freezer paper.

From assorted tree fabrics:
Using the template, cut 4 Large Trees, 8 Medium Trees, and 16 Small Trees.

From tree background fabric:
Cut 1 strip 21½″ × WOF, 2 strips 10¾″ × WOF, 2 strips 5½″ × WOF, 2 strips 5¼″ × WOF, 2 strips 4″ × WOF, and 2 strips 2″ × WOF.

From tree trunk fabric:
Cut 1 strip 3″ × WOF, 1 strip 2½″ × WOF, and 1 strip 1½″ × WOF.

From both snowflake background fabrics:
Cut 2 strips 6″ × WOF. Subcut one of the colors into 10 squares 6″ × 6″ and the other into 12 squares 6″ × 6″.

From sashing fabric:
Cut 3 strips 1″ × WOF. Subcut into 4 rectangles 1″ × 9½″ and 12 rectangles 1″ × 4½″.

Cut 15 strips 1½″ × WOF. From strips, cut 10 strips 1½″ × 26″. Set remainder of strips aside.

Cut 7 strips 4¼″ × WOF.

From top and bottom border fabric:
Cut 4 strips 2¼″ × WOF.

From binding fabric:
Cut 8 strips 2¼″ × WOF.

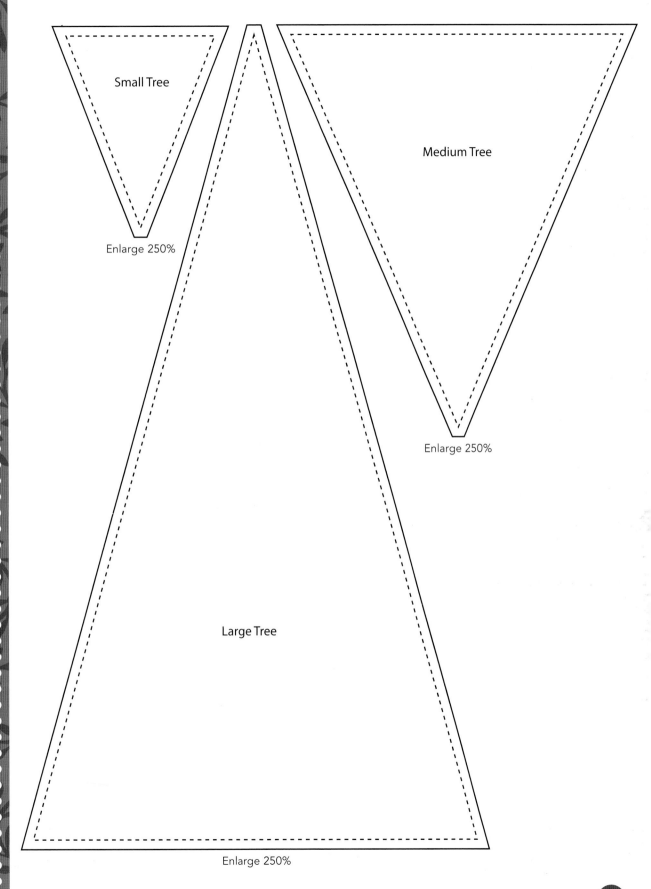

Small Tree

Enlarge 250%

Medium Tree

Enlarge 250%

Large Tree

Enlarge 250%

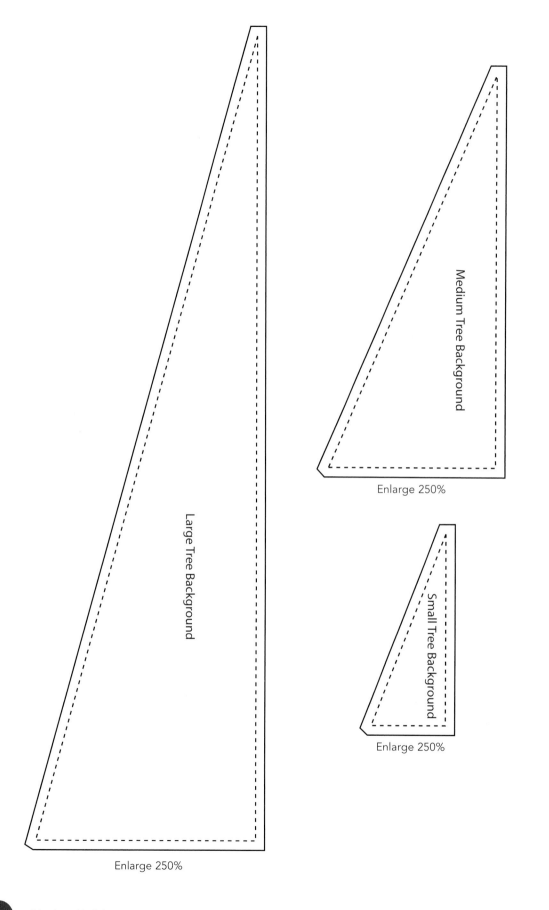

Large Tree Background

Enlarge 250%

Medium Tree Background

Enlarge 250%

Small Tree Background

Enlarge 250%

Tree Block Assembly

1. To make the large trunks, join a 5¼″ × WOF tree block background strip to the long edge of a 3″ × WOF trunk strip. Sew another 5¼″ × WOF tree block background strip onto the other side of the trunk strip as shown. Subcut into 4 units 5″ wide. **FIGURE ❶**

2. To make the medium trunks, join a 4″ × WOF tree block background strip to the long edge of a 2½″ × WOF trunk strip. Sew another 4″ × WOF tree block background strip onto the other side of the trunk strip. Subcut into 8 units 2¾″ wide.

3. To make the small trunks, join a 2″ × WOF tree block background strip to the long edge of a 1½″ × WOF trunk strip. Sew another 2″ × WOF tree block background strip onto the other side of the trunk strip. Subcut into 16 units 1½″ wide.

4. From 21½″ × WOF tree background strip still folded in half so the selvages meet, cut 8 large tree background pieces as shown. (Cutting through both pieces will yield a right and left background piece for the tree.) Trim corners. **FIGURE ❷**

5. From 10¾″ × WOF tree background strips, cut 16 medium tree background pieces in a similar manner.

6. From the 5½″ × WOF tree background strips, cut 32 small tree background pieces in a similar manner.

7. Join a large tree background piece to each side of the large trees as shown. Blocks will be 12½″ × 21½″. **FIGURE ❸**

8. Join a medium tree background piece to each side of the medium trees. Blocks will be 9½″ × 10¾″.

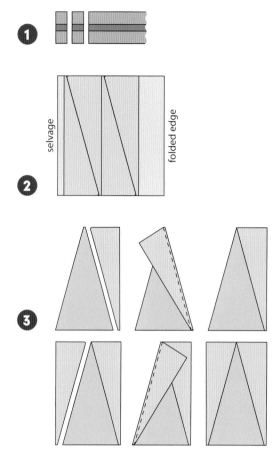

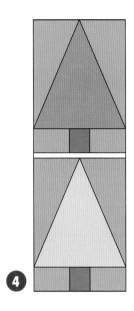

4

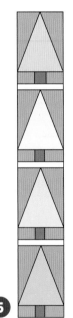

5

9. Join a small tree background piece to each side of the small trees. Blocks will be 4½˝ × 5½˝.

10. Join tree trunks to tree blocks.

11. Join 2 medium tree blocks to a sashing rectangle 1˝ × 9½˝ as shown. Repeat to make 4 units. **FIGURE ❹**

12. Join 4 small tree blocks to 3 sashing rectangles 1˝ × 4½˝ as shown. Repeat to make 4 units. **FIGURE ❺**

Snowflake Block Assembly

1. Enlarge Snowflake Templates (page 133) 120%.

2. Trace 22 snowflakes onto fusible web. Iron onto the wrong side of the white snowflake fabric. Cut out. Remove paper backing and fuse to the center of the 6˝ × 6˝ squares.

3. Back with tear-away stabilizer and machine appliqué each snowflake onto a block, using a buttonhole or zigzag stitch and following tips in the Fusible Appliqué sidebar (page 22).

4. Remove stabilizer and trim blocks to 5½˝ × 5½˝ squares.

Quilt Assembly

1. Referring to the assembly diagram, join snowflake blocks into 2 rows of 11 snow-flakes each, alternating background colors.

2. Join tree block units into rows, inserting a 1½″ × 26″ sashing rectangle between each column of trees.

3. Piece 3 sashing strips 1½″ × 55½″. Lay them out between the tree and snowflake rows, as shown in the assembly diagram. Join rows.

4. Piece 2 sashing strips 4¼″ × 55½″ and join to the top and bottom of quilt top.

5. Piece 2 sashing strips 4¼″ × 72″ and join to the sides of the quilt top.

6. Piece 2 border strips 2½″ × 63″ and join the top and bottom of the quilt top.

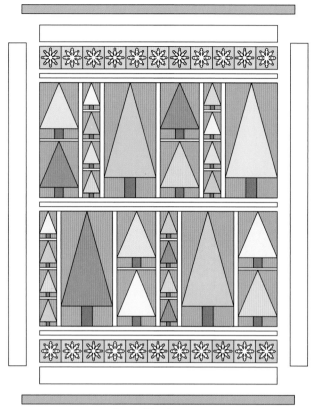

Assembly diagram

Finishing

1. Divide backing fabric into 2 lengths. Cut 1 piece lengthwise to make 2 narrow panels. Join 1 narrow panel to each side of the wide panel. Press seams open.

2. Layer backing, batting, and quilt top. Quilt as desired.

3. Join the 2¼″-wide binding strips into 1 continuous piece for binding. Press, folding in half lengthwise. Sew binding to quilt.

Modern Madness

Finished Quilt:
74˝ × 99½˝

Fabrics shown are from the Flurry collection by Kate Spain for Moda Fabrics.

Pieced by
Amanda Murphy

Quilted by
Deborah Norris

Simple blocks are arranged in a dynamic way to produce a bed-sized design that turns heads! The finished product is well worth the extra layout time. This quilt works best with nondirectional prints. Choose prints that read as solids for the sashing to really make the feature prints pop!

MATERIALS

Block fabrics: ¼ yard of 18 assorted prints
(You will need the full width of the fabric.)

Light sashing, inner border, and accent square fabric:
2 yards

Dark sashing and background fabric: 2½ yards

Outer border and binding fabric: 2 yards

Backing fabric: 6¼ yards

Lightweight fusible interfacing: 1 yard

Batting: 82″ × 107½″ (Warm & Natural batting
by the Warm Company)

CUTTING INSTRUCTIONS

WOF = width of fabric

From block fabrics:
Cut each block fabric into 2 strips 3½″ × WOF. Subcut each
set of strips into 6 rectangles 3½″ × 6½″ and 3 rectangles
3½″ × 9½″.

From light sashing, inner border, and accent square fabric:
Cut 15 strips 1½″ × WOF.

Cut 8 strips 2½″ × WOF.

Cut 5 strips 3½″ × WOF. Subcut into 52 squares 3½″ × 3½″.

From dark sashing and background fabric:
Cut 32 strips 1½″ × WOF. Subcut 8 of these strips
into 80 rectangles 1½″ × 3½″.

Cut 4 strips 9″ × WOF. Subcut into 42 rectangles 3½″ × 9″.

From outer border and binding fabric:
Cut 5 strips 3¼″ × WOF.

Cut 4 strips 5½″ × WOF.

Cut 10 strips 2¼″ × WOF.

From lightweight interfacing:
Cut 16 strips 2″ × WOF.

Sashing Units A and B Assembly

1. Join 2 dark sashing strips 1½″ × WOF to 1 light sashing strip 1½″ × WOF as shown, pressing seams toward dark strips. Repeat to make 10 strip sets. Subcut strip sets into 40 units 5½″ wide and 44 units 3½″ wide. Set the 3½″ units aside—these are Sashing A units. You'll use the 5½″ units to form Sashing B units in Steps 2–4. **FIGURE ❶**

2. Join 1 dark sashing strip 1½″ × WOF to 1 light sashing strip 2½″ × WOF as shown, pressing seams toward light strip. Repeat to make 4 strip sets. Subcut strip sets into 80 units 1½″ wide. **FIGURE ❷**

3. Join a unit from Step 2 to both narrow ends of the 5½″ units from Step 1 as shown, pressing seams toward the outer rectangles. Repeat to form remaining units. **FIGURE ❸**

4. Join a dark sashing rectangle 1½″ × 3½″ to both narrow ends of the unit from Step 3, as shown, to form a Sashing B unit. Press seams toward center of block. Repeat to form remaining units. **FIGURE ❹**

Quilt Assembly

1. Take a deep breath. The trickiest part of this modern design is laying it out. The diamonds look like they are made up of just 1 piece of fabric when in reality they are rectangles from 3 rows of piecing nested together. The entire piece is an optical illusion! You will be laying out the center of this quilt top on a 45° angle.

2. Carefully following assembly diagram 1, lay out the Sashing Units A and B with your block rectangles to form the center of the quilt.

3. Join blocks into rows, pressing seams away from light accent squares, toward Sashing A units, and away from Sashing B units. (This will ensure that the seams lock in the next step.)

4. Join rows.

5. Trim quilt center down to 66½″ × 85½″, following assembly diagram 2 and making sure to center the design. (My side cutting lines were 1½″ away from the outermost diamonds on the quilt.)

6. Turn the quilt top over. Being careful not to stretch the edges of the quilt, apply interfacing along the perimeter, flush with the quilt top's edge. This will stabilize the exposed bias edges before adding borders.

7. Piece 2 inner border strips 1½″ × 85½″ and sew onto each side of the quilt top. Piece 2 inner border strips 2½″ × 68½″ and sew onto the top and bottom of the quilt top.

8. Piece 2 outer border strips 3¼″ × 89½″ and sew onto each side of the quilt top. Piece 2 outer border strips 5½″ × 74″ and sew onto the top and bottom of the quilt top. **FIGURES ❺ AND ❻**

Finishing

1. Divide backing fabric into 2 lengths. Cut 1 piece lengthwise to make 2 narrow panels. Join 1 narrow panel to each side of the wide panel. Press seams open.

2. Layer backing, batting, and quilt top. Quilt as desired.

3. Join the 2¼″-wide binding strips into 1 continuous piece for binding. Press, folding in half lengthwise. Sew binding to quilt.

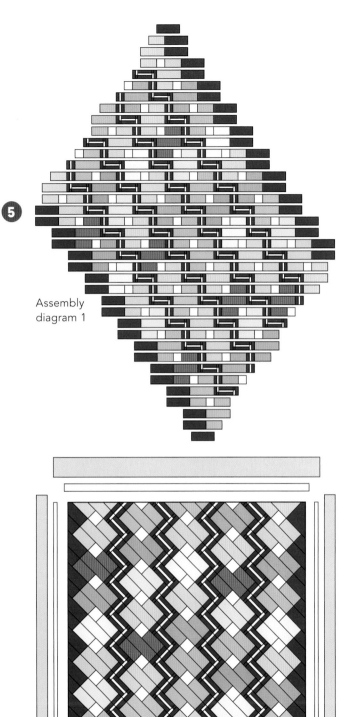

❺ Assembly diagram 1

❻ Assembly diagram 2

Snowfall

Finished Blocks:
8″ × 8″

Finished Quilt:
76½″ × 92½″

Most of the fabrics
shown are from the Brrr!
collection by Laurie
Wisbrun for Robert
Kaufman Fabrics.
The white and the
aqua dotted prints
are Mixmasters by
Patrick Lose for Robert
Kaufman Fabrics.

Pieced by
Amanda Murphy

Quilted by
Deborah Norris

Let your favorite fabrics sparkle like frost on

windowpanes in this fun fat quarter–friendly quilt!

MATERIALS

Snowflakes: 16 fat quarters

Accent squares: ⅝ yard

Background fabric: 4½ yards

Inner border fabric: ½ yard

Middle border fabric: ½ yard

Outer border fabric: 1¾ yards (2¼ yards for a directional print)

Binding fabric: ¾ yard

Backing fabric: 6 yards

Batting: 84½″ × 100½″ (Warm & White batting by the Warm Company)

CUTTING INSTRUCTIONS
WOF = width of fabric

From each snowflake fat quarter fabric:
Cut *widthwise* as shown into 2 strips 5¼″ × WOF and 3 strips 2½″ × WOF. Subcut 5¼″ strips into 4 squares 5¼″ × 5¼″. Subcut 2½″ strips into 16 squares 2½″ × 2½″.

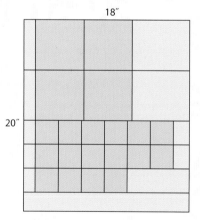

From accent square fabric:
Cut 13 strips 1½″ × WOF. Subcut into 320 squares 1½″ × 1½″.

From background fabric:
Cut 20 strips 2⅞″ × WOF. Subcut into 252 squares 2⅞″ × 2⅞″.

Cut 16 strips 4½″ × WOF. Subcut into 252 rectangles 2½″ × 4½″.

Cut 2 strips 8½″ × WOF. Subcut into 32 rectangles 2½″ × 8½″.

Cut 1 strip 2½″ × WOF. Subcut into 4 squares 2½″ × 2½″.

From inner border fabric:
Cut 8 strips 1½″ × WOF.

From middle border fabric:
Cut 8 strips 1½″ × WOF.

From outer border fabric:
Cut 9 strips 6½″ × WOF. *Note: If you are using a directional fabric, like the one shown, cut 4 strips. Then turn the fabric lengthwise and cut the rest of the strips.*

From binding fabric:
Cut 10 strips 2¼″ × WOF.

Snowflake Block Assembly

1. Use 1 snowflake square 5¼″ × 5¼″ and 4 background squares 2⅞″ × 2⅞″ to make 4 Flying Geese units, following the instructions (page 15) and pressing seams toward geese. Repeat with all remaining 5¼″ × 5¼″ snowflake squares and 2⅞″ × 2⅞″ background squares to complete Flying Geese.

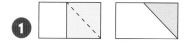

2. Draw a diagonal line on the back of all 2½″ × 2½″ snowflake squares. *With directional prints, orient half of the diagonal lines one way and half the other.*

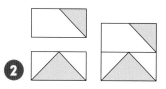

3. Place a 2½″ × 2½″ snowflake square on top of a 2½″ × 4½″ background rectangle, right sides together as shown. Stitch them together, following the diagonal line. Trim seam allowance to ¼″ and press toward the snowflake fabric. Repeat to sew together all 2½″ × 2½″ snowflake squares with the 2½″ × 4½″ background rectangles. **FIGURE ❶**

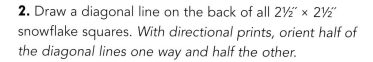

4. Join each Flying Geese unit with a matching unit from Step 3 as shown, pressing seams in a direction that follows that of the seams of the geese units. Twirl the fabric seams in the intersection where they all meet and press for a flat finish. **FIGURE ❷**

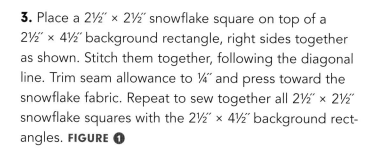

5. Join 4 of these units together to form a Snowflake block as shown. **FIGURE ❸**

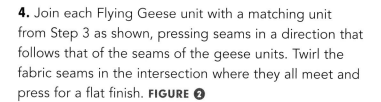

6. Draw a diagonal line on the back of each 1½″ × 1½″ accent square.

7. Place a 1½″ × 1½″ accent square on top of each corner of the Snowflake blocks as shown. Stitch together, following the diagonal lines. Trim seam allowances to ¼″ and press open. Repeat to attach accent squares to all 4 corners of all Snowflake blocks. **FIGURE ❹**

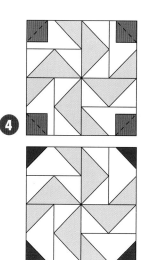

Border Rectangle Block Assembly

Place a 1½″ × 1½″ accent square on top of 2 corners of a 2½″ × 8½″ background rectangle as shown. Stitch together, following the diagonal lines. Trim seam allowances to ¼″ and press open. Repeat to attach accent squares to 2 corners of remaining 2½″ × 8½″ background rectangles. **FIGURE ❺**

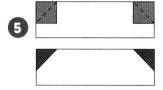

Border Square Block Assembly

Place a 1½″ × 1½″ accent square on top of one corner of each of the 2½″ × 2½″ background squares as shown. Stitch together, following the diagonal lines. Trim seam allowances to ¼″ and press open. Repeat to attach an accent square on the corner of the remaining 2½″ × 2½″ background squares. **FIGURE ❻**

Quilt Assembly

1. Following the assembly diagram, lay 9 rows of 7 blocks each to form the center of the quilt top. Lay a border rectangle block on both ends of each row.

2. Continuing to follow the assembly diagram, use border square blocks and remaining border rectangle blocks to lay a border row on the top and bottom of the quilt top.

3. Join blocks into rows.

4. Join rows.

5. My quilt top at this point was 60½″ × 76½″. Measure your quilt and adjust the border measurements that follow accordingly.

6. Piece 2 inner border strips 1½″ × 76½″ and sew onto each side of the quilt top. Piece 2 inner border strips 1½″ × 62½″ and sew onto the top and bottom of the quilt top.

7. Piece 2 middle border strips 1½˝ × 78½˝ and sew onto each side of the quilt top. Piece 2 middle border strips 1½˝ × 64½˝ and sew onto the top and bottom of the quilt top.

8. Piece 2 outer border strips 6½˝ × 80½˝ and sew onto each side of the quilt top. Piece 2 outer border strips 6½˝ × 76½˝ and sew onto the top and bottom of the quilt top.

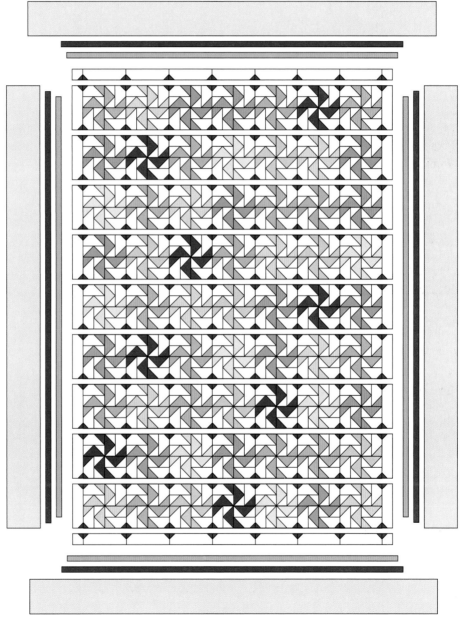

Assembly diagram

Finishing

1. Divide backing fabric into 2 lengths. Cut 1 piece lengthwise to make 2 narrow panels. Join 1 narrow panel to each side of the wide panel. Press seams open.

2. Layer backing, batting, and quilt top. Quilt as desired.

3. Join the 2¼˝-wide binding strips into 1 continuous piece for binding. Press, folding in half lengthwise. Sew binding to quilt.

When you have featured a particularly fun fabric motif in your project, like Laurie Wisbrun's polar bears, it is fun to enlarge it and incorporate it in your quilt label.

Bloom

Finished Quilt:
66″ × 66″

Fabrics shown are from Joy by Kate Spain for Moda Fabrics.

Pieced by
Amanda Murphy

Quilted by
Deborah Norris

Juxtapose modern fabrics in a traditional setting to create this show-stopping quilt! Add detail to the central appliqué panel with hand embroidery in thick perle cotton or free-motion quilting in metallic thread.

MATERIALS

Sashing fabric: 1¼ yards

Poinsettia appliqué fabrics: 1 square 19½″ × 19½″ of light blue background fabric and dark red fabric, 3–5 fat quarters of medium to light red fabrics, and 1 square 6″ × 6″ scrap each of white and green fabric for flower center

Border fabric: 1½ yards

Central panel fabrics: 6 light fat quarters and 3 red fat quarters

Square blocks on the outside of the quilt: 20 squares 8″ × 8″ of assorted prints

Binding fabric: ⅝ yard

Backing fabric: 4⅓ yards

Paper-backed fusible web: 2 yards

Tear-away stabilizer: 1½ yards Sulky Tear-Easy

Batting: 74″ × 74″ (Warm & Natural batting by the Warm Company)

CUTTING INSTRUCTIONS

WOF = width of fabric

From sashing fabric:
Cut 10 strips 2″ × WOF. Piece 2 strips 2″ × 41″ and 2 strips 2″ × 66″. From remaining strips, subcut 16 rectangles 2″ × 9½″.

Cut 7 strips 2½″ × WOF. Piece 2 strips 2½″ × 41″ and 2 strips 2½″ × 66″. From the remaining strips, subcut 4 rectangles 2½″ × 9½″.

From border fabric:
Cut 3 strips 2½″ × WOF for the poinsettia border. Subcut into 2 strips 2½″ × 18½″ and 2 strips 2½″ × 22½″.

Cut 5 strips 2″ × WOF for the central panel border. Subcut into 2 strips 2″ × 38″ and 2 strips 2″ × 41″. *Depending on the fabric width, you may have to piece these bigger strips using the fifth strip.*

Cut 18 strips 1¼″ × WOF for the borders surrounding the big outside squares. Subcut into 40 rectangles 1¼″ × 8″ and 40 rectangles 1¼″ × 9½″.

From central panel fat-quarter fabrics:
Note: Turn all the fat quarters lengthwise to cut the following:

Choose a light fabric for the side, top, and bottom units adjacent to the Poinsettia block and cut 4 strips 4½″. Subcut into 4 strips 4½″ × 18½″.

Choose a light fabric for the corners outside the Poinsettia block and cut 2 strips 4½″. Subcut into 4 rectangles 4½″ × 2½″ and 4 rectangles 4½″ × 6½″.

Cut 2 strips 4⅝″ from each of the remaining light fat quarters. Subcut 4 squares 4⅝″ × 4⅝″ from each fabric.

Cut 1 strip 4¼″ and 2 strips 4⅝″ from one of the red fat quarters. Subcut into 4 squares 4¼″ × 4¼″ and 4 squares 4⅝″ × 4⅝″.

Cut 2 strips 4⅝″ from each of the remaining red fat quarters. Subcut 3 squares 4⅝″ × 4⅝″ from each strip.

From binding fabric:
Cut 8 strips 2¼″ × WOF.

Poinsettia Appliqué Units

1. Enlarge the Poinsettia Template (page 66) to 300%. (*Note: The "vein" markings are optional; see Step 2.*) Following the directions for Fusible Appliqué (page 22), trace the largest poinsettia shape onto the wrong side of the dark red fabric, cut out, and fuse onto the light blue background square 19½″ × 19½″. Back with stabilizer and secure with a blanket stitch or satin stitch. Cut out background fabric layer from beneath the appliqué to prevent fabric layers from becoming too thick. Trace flower petal shapes onto fusible web. Fuse shape 1A onto the wrong side of the lightest of the red fabrics, shapes 2A–2F to the next lightest, and shapes 3A–3F to the third lightest. Fuse the flower center shape onto the wrong side of the white fabric and the flower stamen shape to the wrong side of the green fabric. Cut out. Arrange all pieces on the Poinsettia block, adjusting their placement until you are satisfied. Back with stabilizer and secure each piece with a blanket stitch or satin stitch. Tear away the stabilizer and cut extra fabric from the back of each petal, being careful not to cut the petals themselves.

2. Add hand embroidery, if desired, to show petal veins, or trace the vein shapes onto paper-backed fusible web and fuse to the wrong side of lighter shades of red fabric, if desired. Fuse veins to the Poinsettia block, back with stabilizer, and secure with a narrow zigzag stitch with matching red thread. I used Stitch #2 on my Bernina 580e with a stitch length of 0.9 and a stitch width of 1.2. Remove stabilizer and trim block to a square 18½″ × 18½″. *Another option is to add the veins with thread during the quilting process.*

3A

3B

2B

2A

2C

3F

1A

3C

2F

2D

2E

3E

3D

Poinsettia

Enlarge 300%

Central Panel Units

1. Join light 4½″ × 2½″ rectangles to each narrow end of 2 green 4½″ × 18½″ strips to create 2 A units as shown in **FIGURE ❶**.

2. Join a light 4½″ × 6½″ rectangle to each narrow end of 2 green 4½″ × 18½″ strips to create 2 B units as shown in **FIGURE ❷**.

3. Following the directions, use the 32 light and red squares 4⅝″ × 4⅝″ to make 32 red and light 4¼″ half-square triangle units (below).

4. Join 4 sets of 8 half-square triangles together to create 2 C units as shown in **FIGURE ❸**. *Note that the 2 center red triangles in each unit should match the 4 red squares 4¼″ × 4¼″ that you cut in an earlier step.*

Half-Square Triangle

Refer to the project instructions for the size of the squares.

1. With right sides together, pair 2 squares. Lightly draw a diagonal line from one corner to the opposite corner on the wrong side of one square. **FIGURE ❹**

Draw line.

2. Sew a scant ¼″ seam on each side of the line. **FIGURE ❺**

Sew.

3. Cut on the drawn line. **FIGURE ❻**

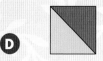

4. Press seams open, and trim off the dog ears. **FIGURE ❼**

Square Block Border Units

1. Following **FIGURE ④**, join a 1¼″ × 8″ border rectangle onto each side of each 8″ square. Join a 1¼″ × 9½″ border rectangle to the top and bottom of each unit.

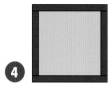

2. Join 4 square blocks together, with a 2″ × 9½″ sashing rectangle between each to create 2 D units as shown in **FIGURE ⑤**. Repeat to make 2 sets.

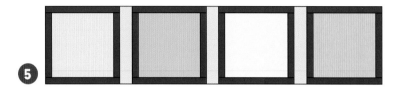

3. Join 6 square blocks together, with a 2″ × 9½″ sashing rectangle between each to create 2 E units as shown in **FIGURE ⑥**. Sew a 2½″ × 9½″ rectangle onto each end of these units. Repeat to make 2 sets.

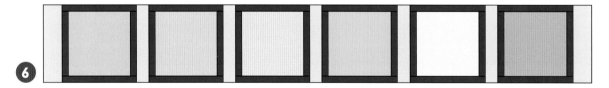

Central Panel Assembly

1. Following assembly diagram 1 join a 2½″ × 18½″ border strip to the sides of the Poinsettia block. Join a 2½″ × 22½″ border strip to the top and bottom of the Poinsettia block.

2. Join the 2 A units to the sides of the Poinsettia block. Join the 2 B units to the top and bottom of the Poinsettia block.

3. Join 2 C units to the sides of the Poinsettia block. Join a red 4¼″ × 4¼″ square to the end of the remaining 2 C units and sew the units to the top and bottom of the Poinsettia block.

4. Join the border 2″ × 38″ strips to the sides of the Poinsettia block and border 2″ × 41″ strips to the top and bottom of the Poinsettia block.

5. You have finished the quilt top center!

Assembly diagram 1

Quilt Assembly

1. Following assembly diagram 2, join a 2″ × 41″ sashing strip to each side of quilt top center.

2. Join a D unit to each side of the quilt top center.

3. Join a 2½″ × 41″ sashing strip to each side of quilt top center.

4. Join a 2″ × 66″ sashing strip to the top and bottom of the quilt top center.

5. Join an E unit to the top and bottom of the quilt top center.

6. Join a 2½″ × 66″ sashing strip to the top and bottom of the quilt top center.

Assembly diagram 2

Finishing

1. Divide backing fabric into 2 lengths. Cut 1 piece lengthwise to make 2 narrow panels. Join 1 narrow panel to each side of the wide panel. Press seams open.

2. Layer backing, batting, and quilt top. Quilt as desired.

3. Join the 2¼˝-wide binding strips into 1 continuous piece for binding. Press, folding in half lengthwise. Sew binding to quilt.

Trimming the Tree

Finished Ornaments:
15″ circles

Finished Quilt:
51″ × 75″

Fabrics shown are from Pink Light Design and Patrick Lose for Robert Kaufman Fabrics and other coordinates by Robert Kaufman.

Pieced by
Amanda Murphy

Quilted by
Deborah Norris
and Amanda
Murphy

Pick a favorite Christmas print and a couple of coordinating small-scale prints for your background. Use complementary solids (or some simple fabrics that read as such) to piece vibrant, oversized ornaments. Appliqué your creations onto the background and create your own unique holiday masterpiece!

MATERIALS

Main background fabric: 3¼ yards

Assorted coordinating background fabrics:
¼-yard cuts of 8–10 coordinating prints
(*You will need the full width of the fabric.*)

Ornaments: 10–12 fat quarters in solids or very simple prints

Letters fabric: 1 fat quarter

Top and bottom border fabric: ¾ yard

Binding fabric: ⅝ yard

Backing fabric: 4¾ yards

Paper-backed fusible web: ¼ yard

Tear-away stabilizer: ¼ yard Sulky Tear-Easy

Decorative thread for hand-quilting the trapunto ornaments (YLI Shimmer in Red and Meadow Green and YLI Candlelight in Medium Blue) and a chenille needle

Grosgrain ribbon ¼˝: 4 yards, *soaked in hot water to preshrink and air-dried*

Batting: 59˝ × 83˝ (Warm & White batting by the Warm Company)

Polyester or wool high-loft batting: 1 yard (*optional*)

CUTTING INSTRUCTIONS

WOF = width of fabric

From main background fabric:
Cut 6 strips 1˝ × WOF, 8 strips 1½˝ × WOF, 1 strip 1¾˝ × WOF, 4 strips 2˝ × WOF, 1 strip 2½˝ × WOF, 1 strip 3˝ × WOF, 3 strips 3½˝ × WOF, 2 strips 4˝ × WOF, 2 strips 4½˝ × WOF, 1 strip 4¾˝ × WOF, 2 strips 6½˝ × WOF, and 1 strip 7½˝ × WOF.

From assorted coordinating background fabrics:
Cut 1 strip 1¾˝ × WOF, 1 strip 2˝ × WOF, 1 strip 2½˝ × WOF, 1 strip 3˝ × WOF, 3 strips 3½˝ × WOF, 2 strips 4˝ × WOF, 2 strips 4½˝ × WOF, 1 strip 4¾˝ × WOF, 2 strips 6½˝ × WOF, and 1 strip 7½˝ × WOF.

From border fabric:
Cut 2 strips 3¼˝ × WOF. Cut 2 strips 7¾˝ × WOF.

From binding fabric:
Cut 7 strips 2¼˝ × WOF.

Background Assembly

1. From background strips, piece 3 strips 1″ × 51″, 6 strips 1½″ × 51″, and 2 strips 2″ × 51″.

2. Trim the selvage off the remaining main background strips and coordinating background strips. Orient the strips so that the main fabric is upright and on the left and the coordinating fabric is on the right. Join each remaining main background strip to a coordinating background fabric of the identical width.

3. *Roughly* following the background assembly diagram, arrange these strips in rows to form the quilt top, staggering them so that the coordinates end at different points. *Do not* become wedded to the diagram! If your fabrics are different and your rows need to be rearranged to look their best, do not hesitate to do so.
FIGURE ❶

4. Choose a few rows and pull the coordinating print more toward the center. To do this, trim some of the extra inches from the left end of the main background fabric and sew it to the right end of the strip. This adds interest. If you would like to further shorten the length of some of the coordinating prints, feel free to cut off a few inches.

5. Trim all rows to 51″.

6. Join rows, pressing all seams up.

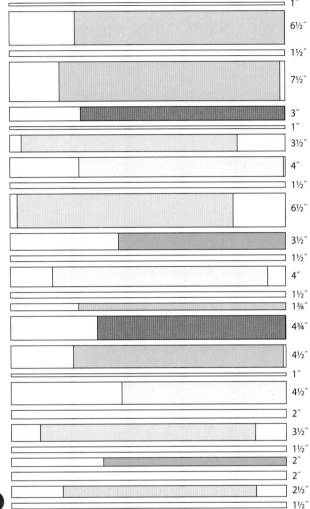

Background assembly diagram

Ornaments

Note: If you are concerned about not having enough fabric, choose three of the fat quarters and set them aside to use for the main fabrics for the Flying Geese ornament, the Pinwheel ornament, and the half-square triangle ornament, respectively.

Flying Geese Ornament

1. Cut 4 squares 5¼″ × 5¼″ from one of your ornament fabrics. Cut 4 squares 2⅞″ × 2⅞″ from each of 4 other ornament fabrics. Following the directions for Easy Flying Geese (page 15), use these squares to make 16 Flying Geese units 2½″ × 4½″.

2. Following the Flying Geese ornament diagram, join Flying Geese together to form 2 rows of 8 geese each.

3. Cut 4 rectangles 1½″ × 16½″ from an ornament fabric that you didn't use for the Flying Geese units. Join to the top and bottom of your Flying Geese rows.

4. Cut 1 rectangle 1½″ × 16½″ and 2 rectangles 2″ × 16½″ from another of the ornament fabrics. Following the Flying Geese ornament diagram, insert the narrow rectangle between the Flying Geese rows and the wider rectangles to the top and bottom of the block. Join rows. **FIGURE ❷**

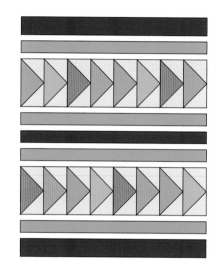

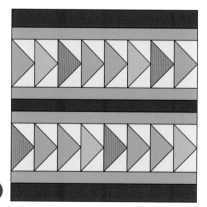

❷

Flying Geese ornament diagram

Pinwheel Ornament

1. Cut 4 squares 1⅞″ × 1⅞″ and 32 rectangles 1½″ × 2½″ from one of your ornament fabrics for your Pinwheel background. Cut 1 square 3¼″ × 3¼″. Cut 4 squares 1⅞″ × 1⅞″ and 4 squares 1½″ × 1½″ from *each* of the other 8 ornament fabrics.

2. Following the directions for Easy Flying Geese (page 15), use the 3¼″ and 1⅞″ squares to make 32 Flying Geese units 1½″ × 2½″.

3. Draw a diagonal line on the back of each 1½″ × 1½″ square. Lay a 1½″ × 1½″ ornament square over a 1½″ × 2½″ background rectangle that you cut in Step 1, making sure to orient the diagonals as shown. Sew on top of the drawn line and trim seam allowance to ¼″. Press the seam open. Repeat to make 32 units. **FIGURE ❸**

4. Join a matching unit from Steps 2 and 3 together as shown. Repeat to make 32 units. **FIGURE ❹**

5. Join 4 matching units from Step 3 together to form a Pinwheel block as shown. Repeat to make 8 Pinwheel blocks. **FIGURE ❺**

6. Join 4 Pinwheels together to make a row. Repeat to make a second row. Join the 2 Pinwheel rows.

7. Cut 4 rectangles 1″ × 16½″ from an ornament fabric that you didn't use for the Pinwheel units. Join to the top and bottom of your Pinwheel unit.

8. Cut 2 rectangles 4″ × 16½″ from another of the ornament fabrics. Following the Pinwheel ornament diagram, join the rows. **FIGURE ❻**

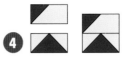

Pinwheel ornament diagram

Mock Hexagon Ornament

1. Cut 2″ strips from a variety of ornament fabrics. (Cut just a few at first, proceed to Step 2, and cut more as needed.)

2. Cut 42 *pairs* of trapezoid shapes using the Mock Hexagon Template.

3. Following the mock hexagon ornament diagram, arrange trapezoids in rows, making sure to position matching trapezoids on top of each other to create the illusion of hexagons.

4. Join blocks into rows, pressing the seams as indicated by the arrows.

5. Join rows. **FIGURE** ❼

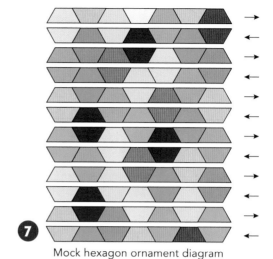

Mock hexagon ornament diagram

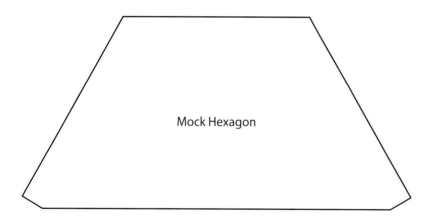

Mock Hexagon

Half-Square Triangle Ornament

1. Cut 32 squares 2⅞″ × 2⅞″ from one of your ornament fabrics. Cut a total of 32 squares 2⅞″ × 2⅞″ from an assortment of other ornament fabrics. Following the directions in the Half-Square Triangle sidebar (page 67), use these squares to make 64 half-square triangles.

2. Following the half-square triangle ornament diagram, join half-square triangles together to form 8 columns of 8 half-square triangles each.

3. Join columns. **FIGURE ❽**

Half-square triangle ornament diagram

Ornament Tops

Following the Fusible Appliqué directions (page 22), trace Ornament Top A Template onto fusible web 4 times and fuse onto the wrong side of the darker of the 2 ornament top fabrics. Trace Ornament Top B Template onto fusible web 20 times and fuse onto the wrong side of the lighter of the 2 ornament top fabrics. Fuse 5 of the light fabric pieces to each dark fabric piece. Back with tear-away stabilizer and secure with a narrow zigzag stitch in a matching thread. Tear off the stabilizer.

Ornament Top A

Ornament Top B

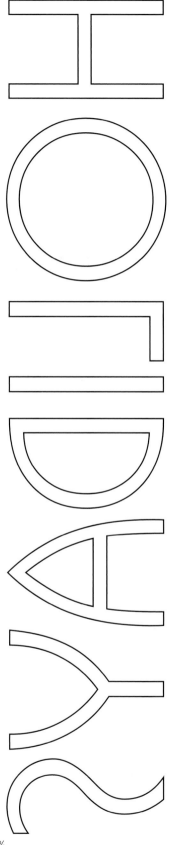

Lettering

Enlarge 250%

Top and Bottom Borders

1. Piece a top border strip 3¼″ × 51″.

2. Piece a bottom border strip 7¾″ × 51″. Following the Fusible Appliqué directions (page 22), enlarge the Lettering Template to 250% and trace onto fusible web. Fuse letter shapes onto the wrong side of the letter fabric. Fuse letters onto bottom border. Back with tear-away stabilizer and appliqué letters with a blanket or satin stitch. Remove stabilizer and trim border to 7¼″ in height.

Quilt Assembly

1. Cut out a 15½″ circle from each ornament block, centering the pieced design.

2. With long (¼″) basting stitches, turn under the outer edge of each ornament ¼″. Press edges to create a smooth circle.

3. Following the assembly diagram, arrange ornaments on top of block in a pleasing manner. Pin.

4. Arrange grosgrain ribbon onto the quilt top to suggest hanging wires. Tuck the bottom raw eges of the ribbon under ornaments and trim top raw edges even with the quilt top. They will be held in place by the top border seam. Baste.

5. Fuse an ornament top on each ornament.

6. Using a blanket stitch and matching thread, appliqué ornaments, ornament tops, and hanging wires onto the background.

7. Sew on the top and bottom borders.

8. If desired, back each ornament with high-loft batting and stitch all the way around the ornament through quilt top and batting as shown in the trapunto technique described on page 37. Cut away excess batting.

Assembly diagram

Finishing

1. Divide backing fabric into 2 lengths. Cut 1 piece lengthwise to make 2 narrow panels. Join 1 narrow panel to each side of the wide panel. Press seams open.

2. Layer backing, batting, and quilt top. Quilt as desired. If you are machine quilting, you might want to hand quilt in the trapunto areas.

3. Join the 2¼˝-wide binding strips into 1 continuous piece for binding. Press, folding in half lengthwise. Sew binding to quilt.

DECORATING YOUR
Home

Three-Dimensional Trees

Made by Amanda Murphy

A holiday forest!

Let your imagination take flight creating a three-dimensional forest. These trees are perfect for gifts or for adorning your mantle or holiday table. The decorating possibilities are endless!

Finished Trees:
large 12″ × 13″
small 9″ × 10″

Fabrics shown are from Alpine Wonderland by Sheri McCulley Studio for Riley Blake Designs.

MATERIALS

Small tree fabric: ¾ yard

Large tree fabric: 1¼ yards

Polyester stuffing

Tree Assembly

1. Decide what size tree you would like to make. If you are making the large tree, enlarge the Tree Template (page 87) 200%. If you are making the small tree, enlarge the Tree Template 150%. (*Note: The dotted lines are just to help you line up and tape the pattern if you are enlarging it.*)

2. Trace the tree pattern onto the dull side of freezer paper. You can reuse the freezer-paper pattern, but if you plan to make a few trees, you may want to trace the pattern a few times.

3. Iron tree pattern onto the wrong side of fabric and cut out. (It helps to place some of the trees upside down or stagger them to fit them all on the fabric.) Repeat to cut 6 tree shapes.

4. Place 2 trees right sides together and stitch around the edge with a scant ¼˝ seam allowance. *Note: Leave 2 openings on the bottom side of the tree as shown, backstitching at the beginning and end of stitching. Repeat 2 times to make 3 tree units.* **FIGURE ❶**

5. Clip seam allowances and turn trees right sides out. Press. Stack trees in a pile, aligning edges. Fold the top tree in half lengthwise and press. Using chalk or a disappearing fabric marker, make a line right down the fold. Place back on top of the pile and pin through all layers. Stitch along the chalk line to join all trees. **FIGURE ❷**

6. Stuff each section of the tree, working from the top branch down. Slipstitch all openings closed.

❶

❷

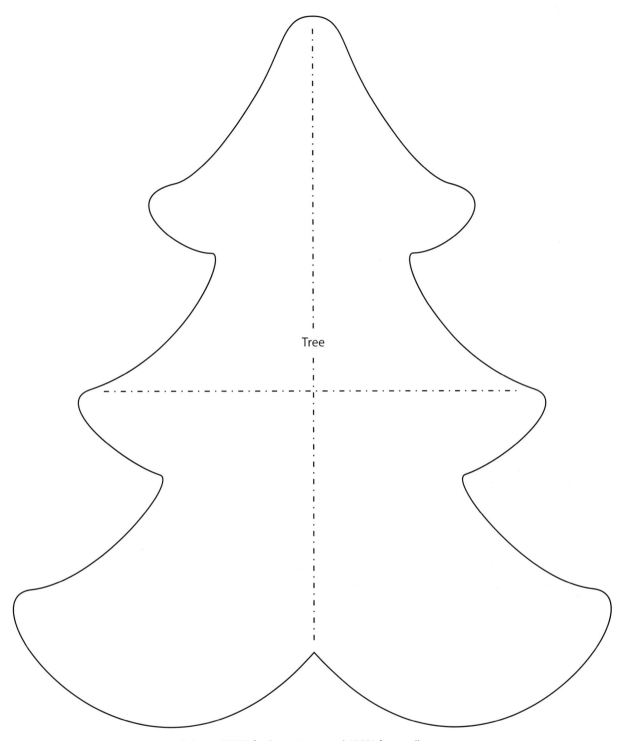

Tree

Enlarge 200% for large trees and 150% for small trees

Modern Ornament Table Runner

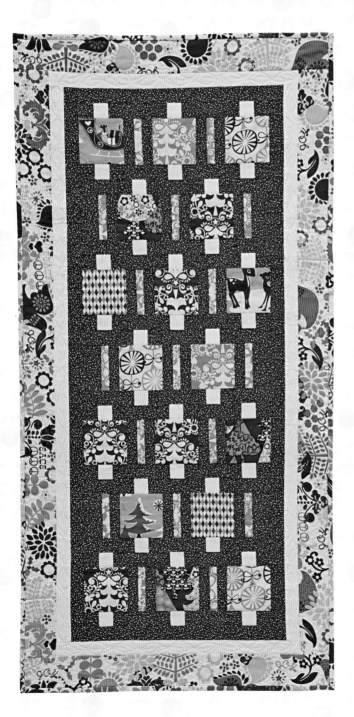

Finished runner: 22″ × 44″

Fabrics shown are from Funky Christmas and other collections by Michael Miller Fabrics.

Pieced and quilted by Amanda Murphy

Let the latest Christmas prints inspire this modern version of a holiday table runner. Your favorite fabrics will lend an element of whimsy to the ornaments that decorate it!

MATERIALS

Ornament fabrics: Assorted prints totaling ½ yard

Ornament accent squares fabric: ⅛ yard

Accent narrow rectangle fabric: ⅛ yard

Background fabric: ¾ yard

Inner border fabric: ¼ yard

Outer border and binding fabric: ¾ yard

Backing fabric: 1½ yards

Batting: 30″ × 52″ (Warm & Natural batting by the Warm Company)

CUTTING INSTRUCTIONS

WOF = width of fabric

From ornament fabrics:
Cut a total of 18 squares 3½″ × 3½″.

From ornament accent squares fabric:
Cut 2 strips 1½″ × WOF.

From accent narrow rectangle fabric:
Cut 2 strips 1″ × WOF.

From background fabric:
Cut 3 strips 1¼″ × WOF, 10 strips 1½″ × WOF, and 1 strip 1¾″ × WOF. Subcut 6 of the 1½″ strips into 2 rectangles 1½″ × 35½″, 2 rectangles 1½″ × 15½″, 12 rectangles 1½″ × 3″, and 22 rectangles 1½″ × 2½″. Set 4 remaining 1½″ strips aside.

From inner border fabric:
Cut 3 strips 1½″ × WOF. Subcut into 2 strips 1½″ × 17½″ and 2 strips 1½″ × 37½″.

From outer border and binding fabric:
Cut 4 strips 2¾″ × WOF. Subcut into 2 strips 2¾″ × 22″ and 2 strips 2¾″ × 39½″.

Cut 4 strips 2¼″ × WOF for binding.

Ornament Block Assembly

1. Join a 1½″ × WOF background strip to each side of each 1½″ × WOF ornament accent square strip as shown, pressing seams toward the background strips. Repeat to make 2 strip sets. Subcut into 36 units 1½″ wide. **FIGURE ❶**

2. Join one of these units to the top and bottom of an ornament square 3½″ × 3½″ as shown. Repeat to make 18 blocks. **FIGURE ❷**

Center Accent Rectangle Block Assembly

1. Join a background strip 1¼″ × WOF to each side of an accent rectangle 1″ × WOF strip as shown. Press seams toward center strip. Subcut the strip into 11 units 3½″ wide. **FIGURE ❸**

2. Join a rectangle 1½″ × 2½″ to the top and bottom of these units as shown, pressing seams toward outer rectangles. **FIGURE ❹**

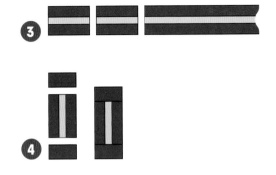

Edge Accent Rectangle Block Assembly

1. Join the remaining background strip 1¼″ × WOF to one side of the remaining 1″ × WOF accent rectangle strip as shown. Join a background strip 1¾″ × WOF onto the other side of the accent rectangle strip. Subcut strip into 6 units 3½″ wide. Press seams toward center strip. **FIGURE ❺**

2. Join a background rectangle 1½″ × 3″ to the top and bottom of these units as shown. Press seams toward outer rectangles. **FIGURE ❻**

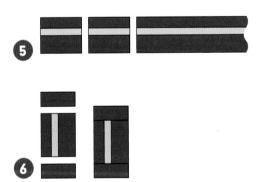

Runner Assembly

1. Join 3 ornament blocks with 2 center accent rectangle blocks to form a row as shown. Repeat to make 4 rows. **FIGURE ❼**

2. Join 2 ornament blocks with 1 center accent rectangle block and 2 edge accent rectangle blocks to form a row as shown. Make sure the sides of the accent rectangle blocks with the wider background strips are oriented outward. Repeat to make 3 rows. **FIGURE ❽**

3. Join rows.

4. Join a 1½″ × 35½″ background strip to each side of the runner top. Join a 1½″ × 15½″ background strip to the top and bottom of the runner top.

5. Following the assembly diagram, join a 1½″ × 37½″ inner border strip to each side of the runner top. Join a 1½″ × 17½″ inner border strip to the top and bottom of the runner top.

6. Join a 2¾″ × 39½″ outer border strip to each side of the runner top. Join a 2¾″ × 22″ outer border strip to the top and bottom of the runner top.

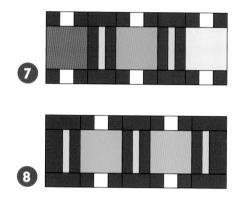

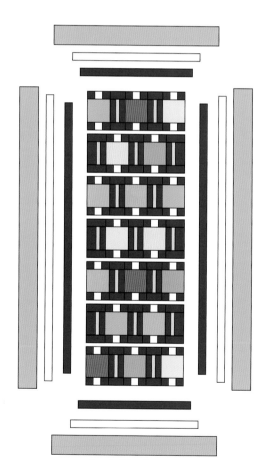

Assembly diagram

Finishing

1. Layer backing, batting, and quilt top. Quilt as desired.

2. Join the 2¼˝-wide binding strips into 1 continuous piece for binding. Press, folding in half lengthwise. Sew binding to quilt.

Countdown to Christmas

Finished Calendar:
23″ × 30″

Fabrics shown are from the Ready Set Snow collection by Me and My Sister Designs for Moda Fabrics.

Pieced and quilted by Amanda Murphy

Select two of your favorite Christmas charm packs and some border and background fabrics, and wrap some fabric gifts for this festive calendar. Top each package with a yo-yo bow as you count down to Christmas!

MATERIALS

Gifts and bow fabric: 2 charm packs or 50 squares 5″ × 5″ of assorted fabrics

Main background fabric: ¾ yard

Accent background fabric for the area beneath the gifts: ¼ yard

Flange strip (between the 2 background fabrics): ⅛ yard

Side border fabric: ¼ yard

Top and bottom inner border fabric: ⅛ yard

Top and bottom outer border fabric: ¼ yard

Lettering fabric: ¼ yard

Paper-backed fusible web: ¼ yard

Tear-away stabilizer: ¼ yard

Appliqué thread to match the lettering fabric: 40- or 50-weight cotton thread

Wide rickrack trim: 1½ yards

Hook-and-loop tape dots ½″: 50

Binding fabric: ¼ yard

Backing fabric: 1 yard

Ultra-firm, heavyweight interfacing, such as Timtex: ¼ yard

Clover small green "Quick" Yo-Yo Maker #8700 (optional but highly recommended)

Batting: 31″ × 38″ (Warm & White batting by the Warm Company)

CUTTING INSTRUCTIONS

WOF = width of fabric

From gift and bow fabrics:
Cut each of 25 of the squares into 1 rectangle 1″ × 5″ and 2 rectangles 2″ × 5″. Set remaining 25 squares aside to use for yo-yo bows.

From main background fabric:
Cut 1 strip 4½″ × WOF. Subcut into 1 strip 4½″ × 20½″.

Cut 1 strip 2½″ × WOF. Subcut into 2 strips 2½″ × 18″.

Cut 3 strips 2″ × WOF.

Cut 1 strip 1½″ × WOF. Subcut into 1 strip 1½″ × 19½″.

Cut 4 strips 1″ × WOF.

From the flange strip fabric:
Cut 1 strip 1″ × 18¼″.

From accent background fabric:
Cut 1 strip 3½″ × 19½″.

From the rickrack trim:
Cut 2 strips 25″ long.

From side border fabric:
Cut 2 strips 2¼″ × WOF. Subcut each strip into 2 strips 2¼″ × 25″.

From top and bottom inner border fabric:
Cut 2 strips 1¼″ × WOF. Subcut each strip into 1 strip 1¼″ × 23″.

From top and bottom outer border fabric:
Cut 2 strips 2¼″ × WOF. Subcut each strip into 1 strip 2¼″ × 23″.

From binding fabric:
Cut 3 strips 2¼″ × WOF.

Block Assembly

1. Join a gift rectangle 1″ × 5″ to a gift rectangle 2″ × 5″. Press seams open. Join an identical 2″ × 5″ gift rectangle to the other side of the 1″ × 5″ gift rectangle. Press seams open. Repeat with remaining fabrics to form 25 gifts.

2. Trim gifts down randomly to different sizes. They should be 2½″ wide and between 2½″ and 3″ high.

3. Chain-piece sides of one side of the gift units to background strips 1″ × WOF, right sides together. Cut background strips flush with gift units. Press seams toward gifts.

4. Repeat to attach background strips to the other side of each gift unit.

5. Using the same technique, chain-piece tops of gift units to background strips 2″ × WOF, right sides together. Cut background strips flush with gift units. Press seams toward gifts.

6. Trim all blocks to 3½″ × 4″.

Yo-Yo Assembly

1. Trace a quarter 25 times onto the heavyweight interfacing. Cut out the circles.

2. *You can make yo-yos the traditional way or use a Clover Yo-Yo Maker.* Without a yo-yo maker, cut out 25 circles 2¾″. To form each yo-yo, sew a ¼″ running stitch around the edge of the circle with a strong thread, like buttonhole thread, turning under the fabric ¼″ as you go. Referring to the photograph below, place a circle of heavyweight interfacing in the center of the fabric before pulling up the threads. Pull up the threads as tightly as possible and tie a knot, but don't clip the threads. **OR** Make a yo-yo using the Clover Yo-Yo Maker, placing the circle of heavyweight interfacing before pulling up the threads and tying the knot.

3. With one end of the thread still in your needle, go down through the yo-yo and make a few stitches to attach the rough side of a hook-and-loop tape dot. *You can also use the Button Sew-On foot on your machine (Bernina #18) to attach the yo-yo to the hook-and-loop tape dot!*

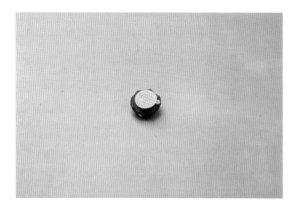

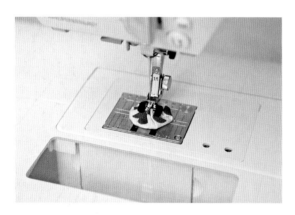

4. Repeat to form 25 yo-yos backed with hook-and-loop tape.

Countdown to Christmas Lettering

1. Trace Lettering Template (page 99) onto the smooth side of the fusible web.

2. Fuse to the *wrong side* of the lettering fabric. Cut out each letter.

3. Remove paper backing from letters. Arrange and fuse onto the background strip 4½″ × 20½″.

4. Back with tear-away stabilizer and machine appliqué lettering onto background, using a thin thread and narrow zigzag stitch the width of the letter stroke.

5. Trim unit to a strip 3½″ × 19½″.

Quilt Assembly

1. Following the assembly diagram, arrange 5 rows of 5 blocks each to form the center of the quilt top.

2. Join blocks into rows.

3. Join rows.

4. Join a background strip 2½˝ × 18˝ to both sides of the calendar unit.

5. Join the lettering unit 3½˝ × 19½˝ to the top of the calendar unit.

6. Join the background strip 1½˝ × 19½˝ to the bottom of this unit.

7. Fold flange strip 1˝ × 19½˝ in half lengthwise and press.

8. Baste flange strip to the right side of one long edge of the accent background strip 3½˝ × 19½˝ using a ⅛˝ seam allowance. Join accent background strip to the bottom of the calendar unit, inserting the flange strip between and aligning raw edges. Press seams toward accent background strip and flange toward the gift blocks.

9. Baste rickrack trim onto sides of quilt top and then join side border strips 2¼˝ × 25˝ to the sides of quilt top. Topstitch rickrack trim along these seams and trim flush with unit.

10. Join top and bottom inner border strips to the top and bottom of the quilt top.

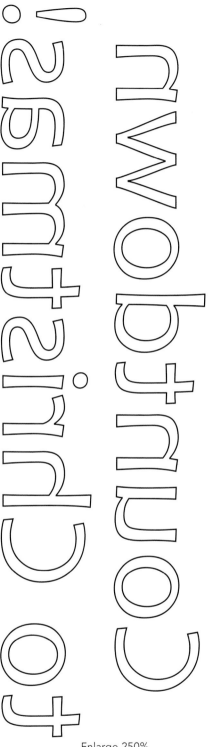

Lettering

Enlarge 250%

11. Join top and bottom outer border strips to the top and bottom of the quilt top.

Attach smooth side of a hook-and-loop tape dot onto the top of each present. (You can do this by hand or use the Button Sew-On foot on your machine!)

12. Following the blue dashed lines on the Countdown to Christmas quilt assembly diagram, draw a horizontal line on the background accent fabric ⅞˝ down from the seam between the flange and background accent fabric and ⅞˝ up from the seam between the background accent fabric and the bottom inner border, using chalk or a disappearing pen. Draw a vertical line through the center of this area. Using sewing thread and small tack stitches through all layers of the quilt sandwich, attach 13 of the smooth hook-and-loop tape dots along the upper line and 12 along the lower line, approximately 1¼˝ apart from each other.

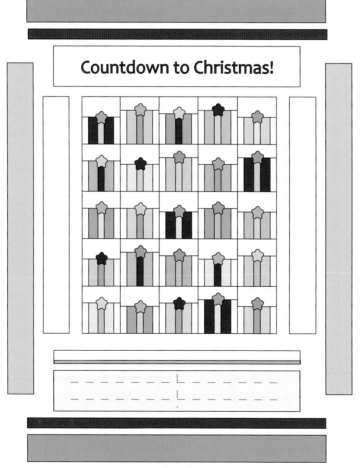

Assembly diagram

Finishing

1. Layer backing, batting, and quilt top. Quilt as desired.

2. Trim excess batting and backing from quilt top.

3. Join the 2¼″-wide binding strips into 1 continuous piece. Press, folding in half lengthwise. Sew binding to calendar.

4. Cut a strip 4½″ × 21″ from unused backing fabric. Sew lengthwise, right sides together, to form a narrow tube. Turn right side out and press seams open. Turn edges of tube under ⅜″. Turn under ⅜″ again and topstitch with a ¼″ seam allowance to secure. Slipstitch hanging sleeve to the top of the calendar.

5. You can inexpensively fashion a hanger for your calendar with a dowel and some pretty ribbon. You are now ready for a Countdown to Christmas!

Christmas Stockings

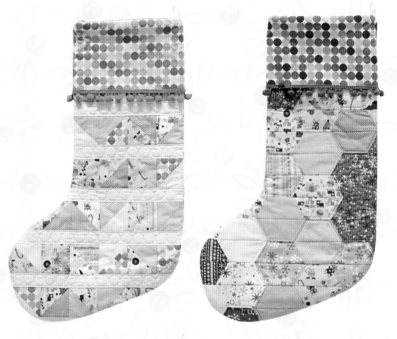

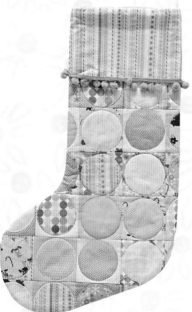

Finished Stocking:
13″ × 21½″

Fabrics shown are from Santa's Workshop by Doodlebug Designs for Riley Blake Designs, adorned with pom-pom trim, also by Riley Blake Designs.

Pieced and quilted by Amanda Murphy

Combine scraps from larger projects to make these fresh, modern stockings. Adorn with pom-pom trim for a whimsical finish.

MATERIALS FOR 1 STOCKING

Stocking top fabric: ½ yard total of assorted scraps

Stocking cuff fabric: 1 rectangle 27″ × 11″

Stocking hanger fabric: 1 rectangle 2″ × 3″

Stocking back fabric: 1 rectangle 16″ × 23″

Lining fabric: ¾ yard

Muslin: 2 rectangles 16″ × 23″

Batting: 2 rectangles 16″ × 23″ Warm & Natural batting by the Warm Company

Pom-pom trim (*optional*): 27″

Stocking Assembly

1. Piece a stocking front that is at least 15″ × 22″ from the choices in the Stocking Front sidebar (page 107).

2. Spread out a rectangle of muslin 16″ × 23″. Layer a piece of batting on top and the stocking front on top. Quilt as desired.

3. Spread out the other muslin rectangle and layer a piece of batting and the stocking back fabric on top. Quilt as desired.

4. Enlarge the Stocking Template to 300%. Keeping the template *right side up*, pin it on top of the stocking front unit and cut out stocking.

5. Turn the template *wrong side up* and place it on top of the stocking back unit. Cut out stocking.

6. Use the Stocking Template to cut out 2 stocking pieces from the lining fabric. One should be right side up and one wrong side up so that the 2 pieces are mirror images of each other.

7. Using a scant ½″ seam allowance, sew the quilted stocking pieces together, leaving the stocking top open. Trim seams to about ¼″. Clip along the curves, almost up to the seamline. Do your best to press the seams open.

8. Using a ½″ seam allowance, sew the lining pieces together, leaving the stocking top open. Clip along the curves, almost up to the seamline. Do your best to press the seams open.

9. Place stocking lining unit inside quilted stocking unit, *wrong sides together*. Pin top of units together, making sure seams match. Baste around top of unit, using a ¼″ seam allowance.

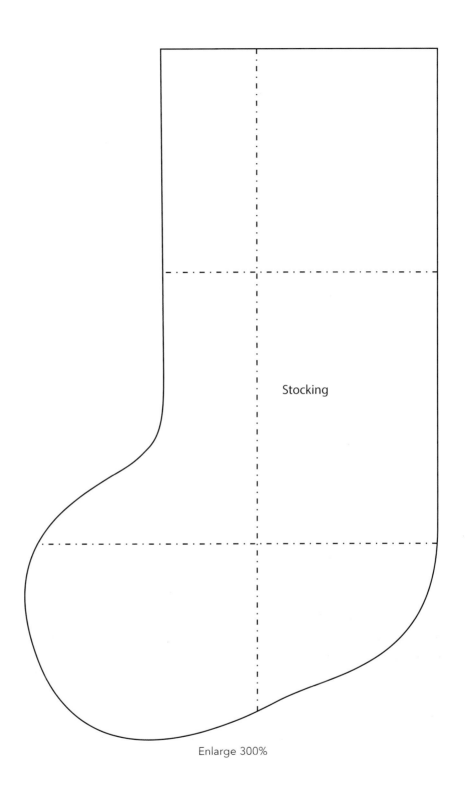

Stocking

Enlarge 300%

10. Fold the 2″ × 3″ hanging loop rectangle in half lengthwise and press. Open fold and fold each side in again, this time so that the raw edge meets the center fold. Fold the 2 halves together. Edgestitch down each side, through all layers of fabric.

11. Fold in half to form a loop and baste to the back side on the inside of the stocking unit, aligning raw edges.

12. Sew short ends of stocking cuff rectangle together. Press seams open. Fold unit in half to form a ring, matching raw edges. Press. Fit cuff inside top of stocking to check fit and adjust if necessary.

13. Pin pom-pom trim to the folded edge of the cuff. Topstitch along the edge to secure.

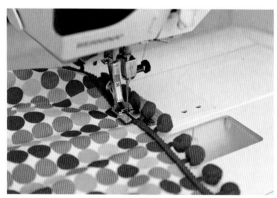

Attaching pom-pom trim with Bernina #38 Piping foot.

14. Pin cuff to stocking top inside lining, right sides together, matching the seam on the cuff to the seam on the side of the stocking. Stitch around the top of stocking through all layers. Fold cuff to the outside and press.

Stocking Front

Vertical Zigzag Stocking

1. Cut 48 squares 2⅞″ × 2⅞″ from a background fabric of your choice. Cut a total of 48 squares 2⅞″ × 2⅞″ from an assortment of other fabrics. Following the directions in the Half-Square Triangle sidebar (page 67), use these squares to make 96 half-square triangles.

2. Following the vertical zigzag stocking diagram, join half-square triangles together to form 8 columns of 12 half-square triangles each.

3. Join columns.

Vertical zigzag stocking diagram

Horizontal Stripe Stocking

1. Cut 8 strips 16½″ × 1½″ from a background fabric of your choice.

2. Cut a total of 56 squares 2⅞″ × 2⅞″ from an assortment of other fabrics. Following directions in the Half-Square Triangle sidebar (page 67), use these squares to make 56 half-square triangles.

3. Following the horizontal stripe stocking diagram, join half-square triangles together to form 7 rows of 8 half-square triangles each.

4. Join rows, alternating half-square triangle rows with background strips.

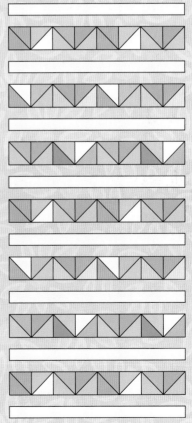

Horizontal stripe stocking diagram

Circle Stocking

Note: You will also need stabilizer, paper-backed fusible web, and heavyweight appliqué thread for this stocking.

1. Cut a total of 40 squares 3½˝ × 3½˝ from a variety of background fabrics.

2. Following the Fusible Appliqué directions (page 22), trace Circle Stocking Template onto fusible web 40 times and fuse onto the wrong side of an assortment of different fabrics. Cut out.

3. Using a blanket stitch and matching (or contrasting!) thread, appliqué circles onto the 3½˝ × 3½˝ background squares, backed with stabilizer. Remove stabilizer after appliquéing.

4. Following circle stocking diagram, join blocks together to form 8 rows of 5 blocks each.

5. Join rows.

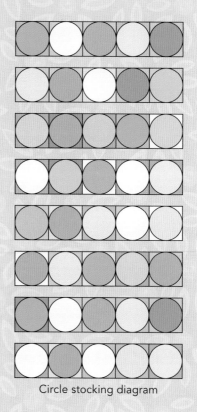

Circle stocking diagram

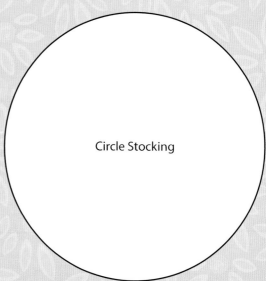

Circle Stocking

Mock Hexagon Stocking

1. Cut a rectangle 16½˝ × 3½˝ from the background fabric of your choice. Cut a few 2˝ strips of background fabric. From strips, cut 33 trapezoid shapes using the Mock Hexagon Template (page 78).

2. Following the mock hexagon stocking diagram, cut 51 more trapezoid shapes using the Mock Hexagon Template from a variety of fabrics.

3. Following the mock hexagon stocking diagram, arrange trapezoids in rows, making sure to position matching trapezoids on top of each other to create the illusion of hexagons.

4. Join blocks into rows, pressing the seams as indicated by the arrows on the mock hexagon stocking diagram.

5. Join rows. Join background rectangle 16½˝ × 3½˝ to the top of the block.

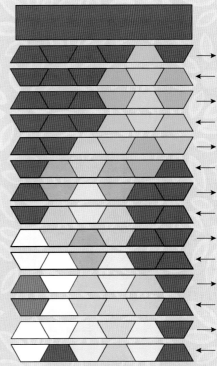

Mock hexagon stocking diagram

Christmas Garland Tree Skirt

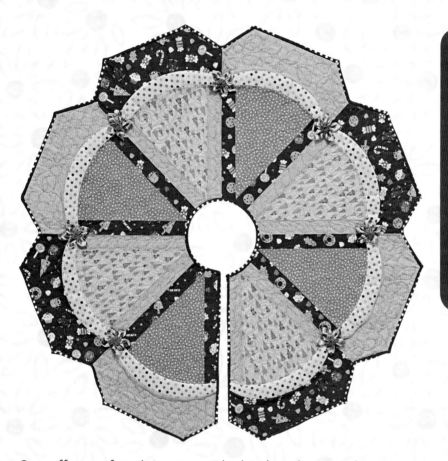

Finished Quilt:
44″ × 44″

Fabrics shown are from Christmas Candy by Doodlebug Designs for Riley Blake Designs, Riley Blenders, and a pink polka-dot print by Deb Strain for Moda.

Pieced by
Amanda Murphy

Quilted by
Deborah Norris

Set off your family's tree with this lovely tree skirt. Clover's Flower Maker makes adding a special touch quick and easy!

MATERIALS

Outer panel green fabric: ¾ yard

Outer panel red fabric: ¾ yard

Inner triangle green fabric: ½ yard

Inner triangle pink fabric (or red coordinate): ½ yard

Garland fabric: ½ yard

Flower fabric: ¼ yard for flower centers and ¾ yard for flower petals

Binding fabric: 1 yard

Backing fabric: 3 yards

Large Clover Flower Maker #8483 or large yellow Clover Yo-Yo Maker #8703

7 decorative buttons or small green "Quick" Clover Yo-Yo Maker #8700

Fusible heavyweight interfacing: ⅜ yard for flowers and yo-yos

Batting: 52″ × 52″ (Warm & Natural batting by the Warm Company)

High-loft batting for trapunto (optional)

CUTTING INSTRUCTIONS

WOF = width of fabric

From each outer panel fabric:
Cut 4 strips 2″ × WOF. Cut these strips in half. Set strips aside. Enlarge the Outer Panel Template, the Inner Panel Template, and the Garland Template 200%. Cut 4 outer panel pieces from the remainder of each outer panel fabric.

From each inner triangle fabric:
Cut 4 inner triangle pieces from each inner triangle fabric.

From binding fabric:
Cut 2¼″ strips *on the bias* for a total of at least 224″. *Do not* try to make the tree skirt using straight-grain binding! You need the bias to nicely finish the inner circle.*

* If continuous bias binding is desired, please consult my blog at amandamurphydesign.blogspot.com or go to tinyurl.com/quiltmaking-basics and download the PDF "How to Finish Your Quilt."

Outer Panel

Enlarge 200%

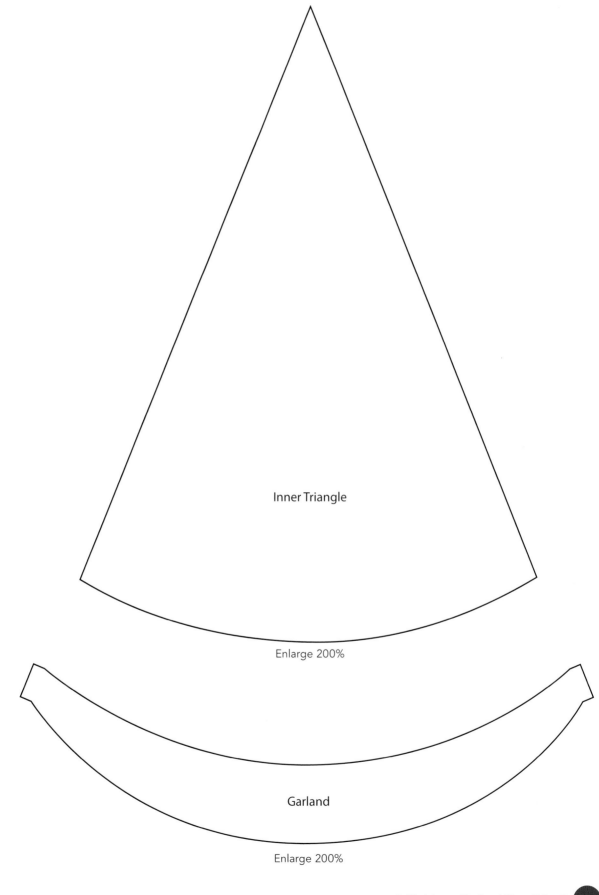

Inner Triangle

Enlarge 200%

Garland

Enlarge 200%

Tree Skirt Top Assembly

1. Join a red 2″ × WOF outer panel strip to a pink inner triangle as shown. Press seams toward strip and trim edge of strip flush with the edge of the triangle. Join a red 2″ × WOF outer panel strip to the opposite edge of the triangle unit. Press seams toward strip and trim edge of strip flush with the edge of the triangle. Repeat to make 4 red/pink triangle units. **FIGURE ❶**

2. In the same manner, join a green 2″ × WOF outer panel strip to a green inner triangle. Press seams toward strip and trim edge of strip flush with the edge of the triangle. Join a green 2″ × WOF outer panel strip to the opposite edge of the triangle unit. Press seams toward strip and trim edge of strip flush with the edge of the triangle. Repeat to make 4 green triangle units.

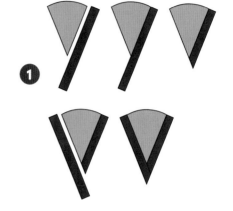

❶

3. Trim a bit off each strip, so the curve of the triangle continues across the top of the units.

4. Join each red triangle unit to a green outer panel unit as shown. **FIGURE ❷**

5. Join each green triangle unit to a red outer panel unit.

6. Trace the Garland Template onto the smooth side of the fusible web 8 times. Cut out the central portion of each garland about ¼″ from its edge so you will be left with only a little fusible in your finished quilt.

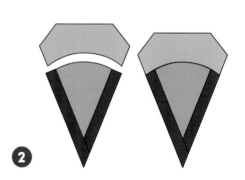

❷

7. Fuse to the *wrong side* of the garland fabric. Cut out.

8. Remove paper backing from garlands and fuse 1 onto the same place on each tree skirt panel.

9. Following the assembly diagram, sew all 8 panels together, matching seams. Leave 1 seam open so you can slip the tree skirt on the tree. Don't fuss too much with the area where all the seams meet in the center. You will be cutting it out before you complete the project.

10. Back with tear-away stabilizer and machine appliqué garlands along the tree skirt using the Fusible Appliqué instructions (page 22). Tear off stabilizer. If desired, back the garland area with high-loft batting using the Trapunto Technique (page 37).

11. Cut a 7″ circle out of the middle of the tree skirt top.

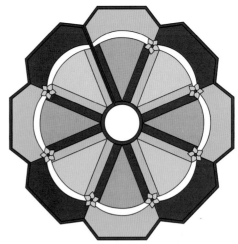

Assembly diagram

Finishing

1. Divide backing fabric into 2 lengths. Join. Press seams open.

2. Layer backing, batting, and quilt top. Make sure the 2 edges of the opening don't overlap. Quilt as desired.

3. Join the 2¼″-wide *bias* binding strips into 1 continuous piece for binding. Starting on a straight side of the tree skirt, sew binding to quilt. Miter the first exterior corner. Turn the quilt top so you are headed to an interior corner.

4. When you get to the first interior corner, stop with the needle down in the seam. Stretch the skirt so that the raw edge of the skirt is lying as straight as you can get it. This means your binding will also lie straight at the pivot point, but the skirt itself will be a little bunched up under the needle. Lower the presser foot and continue to sew about ½″ more along the new side of the quilt. Release the quilt top and sew to the next exterior corner, which you miter in the traditional manner.

5. Apply the rest of the binding in this manner.

6. Once you have applied the binding, clip through the inside corner seam allowances of *only* the binding, right up to, but not through, the stitching line. This is very important. Don't clip through the quilt sandwich!

7. Fold the binding over to the back and hand stitch to secure. I like to put a tiny extra stitch at each of my interior corners through all layers of fabric as I go around the skirt.

8. Following the manufacturer's instructions, make 7 fabric flowers with a yo-yo in the center. Attach at the intersection of the panels and the garlands.

Ornament Pillows

Pieced and quilted by Amanda Murphy

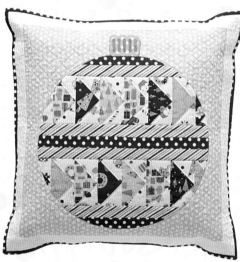 

Put scraps to good use in these lovely Ornament Pillows. They also coordinate beautifully with the *Trimming the Tree* quilt (page 73).

Finished Pillow: 21″ square

Fabrics shown are from Christmas Candy by Doodlebug Design for Riley Blake Designs and Monaluna and Patrick Lose for Robert Kaufman Fabrics. Buttons are by Riley Blake Designs.

MATERIALS

Ornament and ornament top fabric: scraps

Background fabric: 19″ square

Border: ¼ yard

Pillow back fabric: ¾ yard

Binding fabric: ¼ yard

Contrasting buttonhole panel fabric: ¼ yard

Muslin: 22″ square

Batting: 22″ square of Warm & Natural batting by the Warm Company

Buttons, 1″: 3

Fusible interfacing: 2 strips 2″ × 22″

Pillow form: 20″

CUTTING INSTRUCTIONS

WOF = width of fabric

From border fabric:
Cut 3 strips 2¼″ × WOF. From strips, cut 2 strips 2¼″ × 18½″ and 2 strips 2¼″ × 22″.

From pillow back fabric:
Cut 1 rectangle 8″ × 22″ and 1 rectangle 17″ × 22″.

From contrasting buttonhole panel fabric:
Cut 1 strip 4¾″ × 22″.

From binding fabric:
Cut 3 strips 2¼″ × WOF.

Pillow Top Assembly

1. Make an ornament top and your favorite ornament from the *Trimming the Tree* quilt (pages 76–79).

2. Position an ornament top and ornament in the center of the background square. Pin. Using a blanket stitch and matching thread, appliqué onto the background.

3. Trim block to a square 18½″ × 18½″.

4. Following the Ornament Pillow assembly diagram, join a border strip 2¼″ × 18½″ onto the sides of the block.

5. Join a border strip 2¼″ × 22″ onto the top and bottom of the block.

6. Spread out a piece of muslin or scrap fabric that is at least 22″ × 22″ square. (You won't see it in the finished pillow.) Spread a piece of the same size batting on top. Spread the pillow top *right side up* on top of batting and muslin and quilt as desired.

7. Trim quilted pillow top to a 21″ × 21″ square.

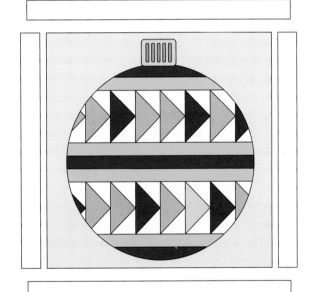

Ornament Pillow assembly diagram

Finishing

1. Join the long edge of the buttonhole panel strip to the long edge of the 8″ × 22″ pillow back rectangle, right sides together. Turn the other long edge of the buttonhole panel under ½″ and press. Fold the buttonhole panel under again lengthwise, wrong sides together, so that the folded edge meets the original seam. Press. Slip an interfacing strip into the buttonhole panel. Press to fuse interfacing. Pin.

2. Turn entire unit right side up and topstitch along the buttonhole panel with matching thread, ⅛″ below the seam that joins the 2 pieces of fabric. *This will secure the folded edge on the back as well.*

3. Sew 1 buttonhole in the center of the buttonhole panel and another 4½″ out from each side of the center buttonhole.

4. Turn under one long edge of the large pillow back rectangle ½″ and press. Turn under the same side 2″ and press. Slip an interfacing strip into this fold and press to fuse.

5. Turn this unit *wrong side up* and topstitch ⅛″ from the edge of the first fold to secure.

6. Baste top and bottom units together as shown in the pillow back diagram, so that the edge of the top unit just overlaps the topstitching on the bottom unit. Open up buttonholes and mark button placement on bottom panel.

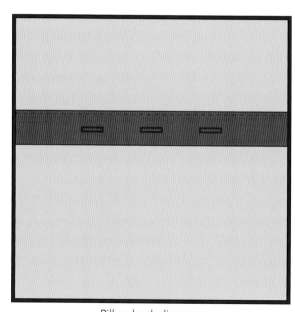

Pillow back diagram

7. Layer quilted pillow top onto back *wrong* sides together and baste ⅛″ from pillow top edge. Trim excess pillow back fabric.

8. Join together binding strips. Fold in half lengthwise and press. Sew binding to the outer edge of the pillow front. Wrap around to pillow back and hand stitch to secure. Remove basting from back panel and apply buttons. Enjoy your lovely Ornament Pillows!

Ornament Pillow backs

Tree Pillows

Finished Pillow: 21″ square

Fabrics shown are from Flurry by Kate Spain for Moda Fabrics and Urban Chiks for Moda Fabrics. Buttons are fabric covered or from Riley Blake Designs.

Pieced and quilted by Amanda Murphy

Put scraps to good use in these lovely Tree Pillows.

MATERIALS

Tree fabrics: scraps

Background fabric: 19″ × 19″ square

Border: ¼ yard

Trim or beads to decorate the tree (*optional*)

Binding fabric: ¼ yard

Pillow back fabric: ¾ yard

Contrasting buttonhole panel fabric: ¼ yard

Muslin: 22″ square

Batting: 22″ square of Warm & Natural batting by the Warm Company

Buttons, 1″: 3

Paper-backed fusible web: ⅓ yard

Tear-away stabilizer: ⅓ yard

Fusible interfacing: 2 strips 2″ × 22″

Pillow form: 20″ × 20″

CUTTING INSTRUCTIONS

From border fabric:
Cut 2 strips 2¼″ × width of fabric. Subcut each strip into 1 rectangle 2¼″ × 18½″ and 1 rectangle 2¼″ × 21½″.

From pillow back fabric:
Cut 1 rectangle 8″ × 22″ and 1 rectangle 17″ × 22″.

From contrasting buttonhole panel fabric:
Cut 1 strip 4¾″ × 22″.

From binding fabric:
Cut 3 strips 2¼″ × width of fabric.

Pillow Top Assembly

1. Cut scraps into strips and piece the block to at least 12″ × 17″ for the tree. The edges don't have to be parallel—a little wonky is good!

2. Enlarge Tree Template (page 126) 200% and trace pieces onto fusible web, following the instructions for Fusible Appliqué (page 22). Fuse onto the wrong sides of the trunk fabric, star fabric, and tree unit. Cut out pieces and position on background square. If desired, hand-baste trim diagonally across the tree to simulate "garlands," tucking raw edges of trim underneath the tree. Fuse all appliqué pieces to the background. Back with stabilizer. Using a satin stitch and matching thread, appliqué onto the background. Remove stabilizer.

3. Trim block to a square 18½″ × 18½″.

4. Following the assembly diagram, join a border rectangle 2¼″ × 18½″ onto the sides of the block.

5. Join a border rectangle 2¼″ × 21½″ onto the top and bottom of the block.

6. Spread out a piece of muslin or scrap fabric that is at least 22″ square. (You won't see it in the finished pillow.) Spread a piece of the same size batting on top. Spread the pillow top *right side up* on top of batting and muslin and quilt as desired, catching optional trim in quilting to secure.

7. Trim quilted pillow top to a 21″ × 21″ square.

8. Add beads or trim to decorate the tree, if desired.

Assembly diagram

Tree

Enlarge 200%

Finishing

Follow the directions for finishing the Ornament Pillow (page 120) to complete your Tree Pillow.

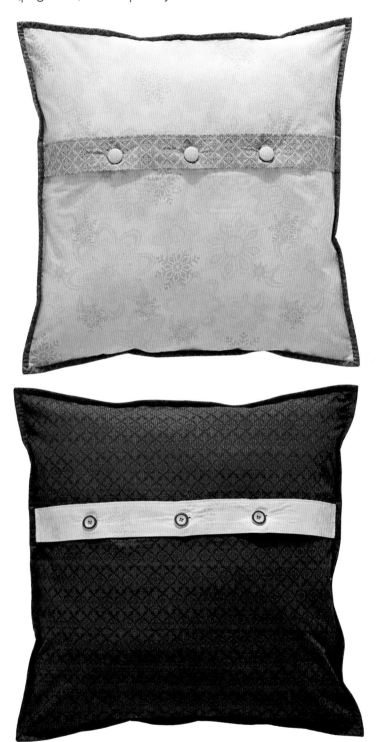

Back of Tree Pillows

Snowflake Pillows

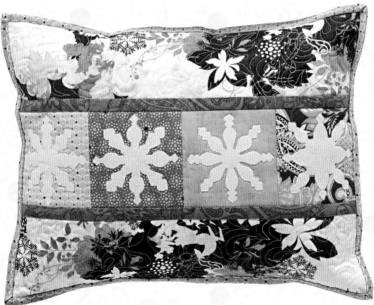

Finished Pillow:
16½″ × 12½″

Fabrics shown are from Blitzen by BasicGrey for Moda Fabrics. Coordinating buttons are also from BasicGrey.

Pieced and quilted by Amanda Murphy

Whip up some festive Snowflake Pillows for your home or for a friend's. The pattern coordinates with the *Holiday Forest* quilt (page 41).

MATERIALS

Main pillow front fabric: ¼ yard

Pillow front accent fabrics: 4 squares 5″ × 5″

Pillow front horizontal trim fabric:
2 strips 16½″ × 1″

Snowflake fabric: ¼ yard

Pillow back fabric: 1 fat quarter

Contrasting buttonhole panel fabric: ¼ yard

Muslin or scrap fabric: rectangle 18″ × 14″

Binding fabric: ¼ yard

Batting: rectangle 18″ × 14″ of Warm & Natural batting by the Warm Company

Buttons, ¾″: 7

Paper-backed fusible web: ¼ yard

Tear-away stabilizer: ¼ yard

Fusible interfacing: 2 strips 2″ × 14½″

Pillow form: 12″ × 16″

CUTTING INSTRUCTIONS

From main pillow front fabric:
Cut 2 rectangles 4½″ × 16½″.

From pillow front horizontal trim fabric:
Cut 2 strips 1″ × 16½″.

From contrasting buttonhole panel fabric:
Cut 1 strip 4¾″ × 14″.

From pillow back fat quarter:
Cut 1 rectangle 12″ × 14″ and 1 rectangle 8″ × 14″.

From binding fabric:
Cut 2 strips 2¼″ × width of fabric.

Pillow Top Assembly

1. Trace 4 snowflakes from Snowflake Template (page 133) onto fusible web (see Fusible Appliqué, page 22). Fuse onto the wrong sides of snowflake fabric. Cut out each snowflake and position on a 5″ × 5″ square of accent fabric. Fuse. Back with stabilizer. Using a blanket or zigzag stitch and matching thread, appliqué onto the background. Remove stabilizer after appliquéing.

2. Trim block to 4½″ × 4½″ square.

3. Following the Snowflake Pillow diagram, join the 4 snowflake blocks in a row.

4. Join a 1″ × 16½″ horizontal trim rectangle onto the top and bottom of this unit.

5. Join a 4½″ × 16½″ main pillow fabric rectangle onto the top and bottom of the pillow top.

6. Spread out the rectangle of muslin or scrap fabric. (You won't see it in the finished pillow.) Spread the rectangle of batting on top. Spread the pillow top *right side up* on top of batting and muslin and quilt as desired.

7. Trim quilted pillow top to a 16½″ × 12½″ rectangle.

Snowflake Pillow diagram

Finishing

Note: This pillow is assembled in a similar manner to the Ornament Pillows (page 120).

1. Join the long edge of the buttonhole panel rectangle to the long edge of the larger pillow back rectangle, right sides together. Turn the other long edge of the buttonhole panel under ½″ and press. Fold the buttonhole panel under again lengthwise, *wrong sides together*, so that the folded edge meets the original seam. Press. Slip an interfacing strip into the buttonhole panel. Press to fuse interfacing. Pin.

2. Turn entire unit right side up and topstitch along the buttonhole panel with matching thread, ⅛″ below the seam that joined the 2 pieces of fabric. (This will secure the folded edge on the back as well.)

3. Make a mark in the center of the buttonhole panel to indicate the central buttonhole placement. Make 3 more marks at 1½″ intervals on both sides of the central buttonhole mark. Stitch a buttonhole at each location.

4. Turn under one short edge of the 12″ × 14″ pillow back rectangle ½″ and press. Turn under the same side 2″ and press. Slip in an interfacing strip into this fold and press to fuse.

5. Turn this unit *wrong side up* and topstitch ⅛″ from the edge of the first fold to secure.

6. Baste top and bottom units together, so that the edge of the top unit just overlaps the topstitching on the bottom unit. Open up buttonholes and mark button placement on bottom panel.

7. Layer quilted pillow top onto back *wrong sides together* and baste ⅛″ from pillow top edge. Trim excess pillow back fabric.

8. Join together binding strips. Fold in half lengthwise and press. Sew binding to the outer edge of the pillow front. Wrap around to pillow back and hand stitch to secure. Remove basting from back panel and apply buttons.

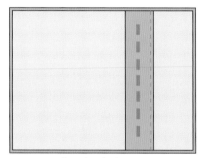

Pillow back diagram

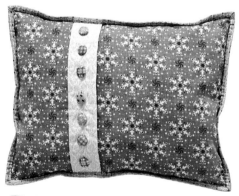

Back of Snowflake Pillows

Snowflake

Snowflake

Snowflake

Snowflake

Snowflake Coasters

Pick a festive holiday charm pack and make a bunch of coasters to give away as holiday gifts, or use scraps you have left over from other holiday projects to make a set for yourself!

Finished Coasters: 5½″ × 5½″ square

Fabrics shown are Santa's Workshop by Doodlebug Design for Riley Blake Designs.

Pieced and quilted by Amanda Murphy

MATERIALS FOR 1 SET OF 4 COASTERS

Snowflake fabric: 4 squares 5″ × 5″

Paper-backed fusible web: 4 squares 5″ × 5″

Background fabric: 4 squares 5″ × 5″

Border fabric: 1 fat quarter

Backing fabric: 4 squares 6″ × 6″

Batting: 4 squares 6″ × 6″ Warm & White batting by the Warm Company

Coaster Assembly

1. Trace snowflakes from Snowflake Template (page 133) onto the smooth side of the paper-backed fusible web. Fuse onto wrong side of snowflake fabric. Cut out snowflakes.

2. Choose 4 squares to use for the coaster backgrounds. Fuse snowflakes onto backgrounds.

3. From border fabric, cut 8 rectangles 1″ × 5″ and 8 rectangles 1″ × 6″.

4. Following the assembly diagram, join a border rectangle 1″ × 5″ onto the sides of each snowflake block. Press out. Join a border rectangle 1″ × 6″ on the top and bottom of the block. Press seams out.

5. Spread out a square of batting. Place a finished snowflake block *right side up* on top. Place a backing square *wrong side up* on top. Using a walking foot, stitch around the coaster using a ¼″ seam allowance, leaving a 3″ opening on one side for turning. Make sure to backstitch on each end. Repeat with remaining coasters.

6. Clip corners and turn coasters right side out. Press. Slipstitch openings closed.

7. Stitch in-the-ditch around each coaster between the border and the background.

8. Change to an embroidery foot and thread that matches the snowflakes, and stitch around the outside of each, staying close to the edge of the fabric.

9. Enjoy a creamy mug of hot chocolate and your lovely coasters with family and friends!

Assembly diagram

QUILTMAKING
Basics

Borders

When you have finished the quilt top, measure it through the center vertically. This will be the length to cut the side borders. Piece the strips together to achieve the needed lengths. Place pins at the centers of all four sides of the quilt top, as well as in the center of each side border strip. Pin the side borders to the quilt top first, matching the center pins. Sew the borders to the quilt top and press toward border.

Measure horizontally across the center of the quilt top including the side borders. This will be the length to cut the top and bottom borders. Repeat, pinning, sewing, and pressing.

Backing

Plan on making the backing a minimum of 8″ longer and wider than the quilt top. Piece, if necessary.

Batting

Most of these quilts feature Warm & Natural or Warm & White cotton batting, although I have used high-loft batting for the trapunto work. Cut batting approximately 8″ longer and wider than your quilt top. Check the manufacturer's instructions to see how far apart the quilting lines can be.

Layering

Spread the backing wrong side up and tape the edges down with masking tape. (If you are working on carpet you can use T-pins to secure the backing to the carpet.) Center the batting on top, smoothing out any folds. Place the quilt top right side up on top of the batting and backing, making sure it is centered.

Basting

Basting keeps the quilt "sandwich" layers from shifting while you are quilting.

If you plan to machine quilt, pin baste the quilt layers together with safety pins placed about 3″–4″ apart.

Quilting

Quilting, whether by hand or machine, enhances the pieced or appliquéd design of the quilt. You may choose to quilt in-the-ditch, echo the pieced or appliqué motifs, use patterns from quilting design books and stencils, or do your own free-motion quilting. Remember to check your batting manufacturer's recommendations for how close the quilting lines must be.

Binding

Trim excess batting and backing from the quilt even with the edges of the quilt top.

If you want a ¼˝ finished binding, cut the binding strips 2¼˝ wide and piece them together with diagonal seams to make a continuous binding strip. Trim the seam allowance to ¼˝. Press the seams open.
FIGURES ❶ AND ❷

Press the entire strip in half lengthwise with wrong sides together. With raw edges even, pin the binding to the front edge of the quilt a few inches away from a corner and leave the first few inches of the binding unattached. Start sewing, using a ¼˝ seam allowance.

Stop ¼˝ away from the first corner (see Step 1) and backstitch one stitch. Lift the presser foot and needle. Rotate the quilt one-quarter turn. Fold the binding at a right angle so it extends straight above the quilt and the fold forms a 45° angle in the corner (see Step 2). Then bring the binding strip down even with the edge of the quilt (see Step 3). Begin sewing at the folded edge. Repeat in the same manner at all corners.
FIGURES ❸ – ❺

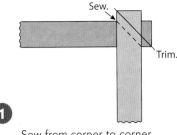

❶ Sew from corner to corner.

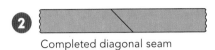

❷ Completed diagonal seam

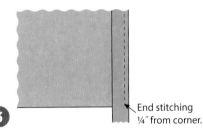

❸ **Step 1.** Stitch to ¼˝ from corner.

End stitching ¼˝ from corner.

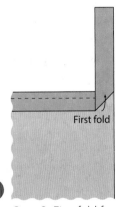

❹ **Step 2.** First fold for miter

First fold

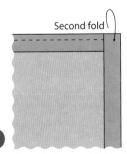

❺ **Step 3.** Second fold alignment

Second fold

Continue stitching until you are back near the beginning of the binding strip. Cut both ends of the binding so that they overlap a scant 2¼˝.

Open both tails. Place one tail on top of the other tail at right angles, right sides together. Mark a diagonal line from corner to corner and stitch on the line. Check that you've done it correctly and that the binding fits the quilt; then trim the seam allowance to ¼˝. Press open. **FIGURE 6**

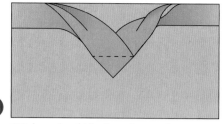

Stitch ends of binding diagonally.

Refold the binding and stitch this binding section in place on the quilt. Fold the binding over the raw edges to the quilt back and hand stitch.

For instructions on making continuous bias binding, please consult my blog at amandamurphydesign.blogspot.com or go to tinyurl.com/quiltmaking-basics and download the PDF "How to Finish Your Quilt."

General Instructions

Seam allowances for all the projects in this book are ¼˝, unless otherwise noted.

WOF stands for *width of fabric*.

All required yardage is based on a fabric width of 40˝.

A *fat quarter* is a quarter-yard piece of fabric obtained by cutting one yard of fabric in half once on its length and again on its width.

Fabric Designer Blog Roll

BasicGrey
blog.basicgrey.com

Deb Strain
debstrain.blogspot.com

Doodlebug Design
doodlebugblog.com

Kate Spain
katespaindesigns.blogspot.com

Laurie Wisbrun
lauriewis.blogspot.com

Me and My Sister
meandmysisterdesigns.com

Monaluna—Jennifer Moore
monaluna.com

Patrick Lose
patricklose.blogspot.com

Piece O' Cake Designs
pieceocake.com

Pink Light Design—Mary Beth Freet
pinkhappythoughtsalways.blogspot.com

Sheri McCulley Studio
sherimcculley.com

Supplies and Sources

Aurifil USA
50-weight cotton piecing thread and 12- and 28-weight cotton thread for appliqué
312-212-3485
aurifil.com

BasicGrey
Buttons
basicgrey.com/fabric
blog.basicgrey.com

Bernina of America, Inc.
Bernina 580e
berninausa.com
WeAllSew.com

Clover
"Quick" Yo-Yo and Flower Makers
clover-usa.com

Creative Grids USA
Rulers
creativegridsusa.com

Deborah's Quilting
Deborah Norris (quilter)
deborahsquilting.blogspot.com

Michael Miller Fabrics
Fabric
212-704-0774
michaelmillerfabrics.com
makingitfun.blogspot.com

Moda Fabrics
Fabric
modafabrics.com
modafabrics.blogspot.com

Riley Blake Designs
Fabric, buttons, and pom-pom trim
801-727-8890
rileyblakedesigns.com

Sulky of America
Sulky Tear-Easy Stabilizer and 12- and 30-weight cotton thread for appliqué
sulky.com

Robert Kaufman Fabrics
Fabric
800-877-2066
robertkaufman.com
swatchandstitch.com

Simplicity
Easy Dresden by Darlene Zimmerman
simplicity.com

Amann USA Embroidery Threads
Yenmet metallic thread
amannusa.com/yenmet

The Warm Company
Warm & White, Warm & Natural, and Lite Steam-A-Seam 2
warmcompany.com

Velcro USA Inc.
Velcro
velcro.com

YLI
Wash-A-Way thread
ylicorp.com

About the Author

Always attracted to color, texture, and pattern, Amanda Murphy has been designing, drawing, and sewing since she was a child. After graduating with a BFA in design from Carnegie Mellon University, she worked as a graphic designer and art director in Alexandria, Virginia, and in New York City. After moving to North Carolina with her family, Amanda discovered quilting, an art that marries her passion for design with her enthusiasm for handwork. As she gradually expanded her knowledge of quilting techniques and combined them with the ideas she had been sketching over the years, Amanda Murphy Design was born.

Photo by Liz Sawyer-Menaker

Amanda markets her own pattern line under the Amanda Murphy Design label and has designed several fabric collections for Robert Kaufman Fabrics and most recently for Blend Fabrics, a subsidiary of Anna Griffin, Inc. Amanda is pleased to announce that Blend Fabrics will produce a line of quilting fabrics called Holiday Bouquet, inspired by her artwork in this book. Look for Amanda's second book with C&T Publishing in the fall of 2013.

Amanda hopes that both her fabric and her quilt designs will inspire others to create their own works of art.

Website: amandamurphydesign.com

Blog: amandamurphydesign.blogspot.com